Accession no.
36139381

D1585090

WITHDRAWN

The Happiness Agenda

The Happiness Agenda

A Modern Obsession

Simon Burnett

LIS - LIBRARY

Date	Fund
18·11·14	h-che

Order No.

2555992

University of Chester

palgrave
macmillan

© Simon Burnett 2012
Foreword © Cary L. Cooper 2012

All rights reserved. No reproduction, copy or transmission of this
publication may be made without written permission.

No portion of this publication may be reproduced, copied or transmitted
save with written permission or in accordance with the provisions of the
Copyright, Designs and Patents Act 1988, or under the terms of any licence
permitting limited copying issued by the Copyright Licensing Agency,
Saffron House, 6–10 Kirby Street, London EC1N 8TS.

Any person who does any unauthorized act in relation to this publication
may be liable to criminal prosecution and civil claims for damages.

The author has asserted his right to be identified as the author of this
work in accordance with the Copyright, Designs and Patents Act 1988.

First published 2012 by
PALGRAVE MACMILLAN

Palgrave Macmillan in the UK is an imprint of Macmillan Publishers Limited,
registered in England, company number 785998, of Houndmills, Basingstoke,
Hampshire RG21 6XS.

Palgrave Macmillan in the US is a division of St Martin's Press LLC,
175 Fifth Avenue, New York, NY 10010.

Palgrave Macmillan is the global academic imprint of the above companies
and has companies and representatives throughout the world.

Palgrave® and Macmillan® are registered trademarks in the United States,
the United Kingdom, Europe and other countries.

ISBN 978–0–230–28956–7

This book is printed on paper suitable for recycling and made from fully
managed and sustained forest sources. Logging, pulping and manufacturing
processes are expected to conform to the environmental regulations of the
country of origin.

A catalogue record for this book is available from the British Library.

Library of Congress Cataloging-in-Publication Data
Burnett, Simon, 1981–
The happiness agenda : a modern obsession / Simon Burnett.
p. cm.
Includes index.
ISBN 978–0–230–28956–7 (hardback)
1. Happiness. 2. Happiness—United States. I. Title.
BF575.H27B87 2011
302'.1—dc23   2011024175

10   9   8   7   6   5   4   3   2   1
21 20 19 18 17 16 15 14 13 12

Printed and bound in Great Britain by
CPI Antony Rowe, Chippenham and Eastbourne

The question is asked, whether happiness is to be acquired by learning or by habituation or some other sort of training, or comes in virtue of some divine providence or again by chance. Now if there is any gift of the gods to men, it is reasonable that happiness should be god-given, and most surely god-given of all human things inasmuch as it is the best.

(Aristotle, 350 BCE)

To Nik

Contents

Foreword
To be or not to be happy!

Cary L. Cooper

The search for the magic bullet of happiness seems to dominate the headlines these days. It started with the King of Bhutan declaring that what was important for his kingdom was national well-being. This was followed by many other leaders, such as Nicholas Sarkozy of France and David Cameron of the UK, the latter suggesting that although GDP is important GNW (Gross National Well-being) was equally important. Indeed, the UK government is canvassing the population at this moment in time to construct some well-being items to include in their annual Office of National Statistics survey to gauge the nation's happiness. In addition, strangely enough, academic economists have taken the lead in arguing that happiness has a substantial "benefit to cost" ratio for society, and that is it not just a soft and fuzzy construct but can have material positive outcomes for individuals, the workplace, communities and the like. Books now abound on the economic and other benefits of a "happy society," with global league tables ranking countries on happiness indices.

There are several difficulties in this movement. First, that there may be a difference between an ephemeral emotional state like happiness, and a more enduring and broader construct like 'well-being'. The two have been merged in the literature and in the public's perception, so some work needs to be done to disentangle these. A person can be happy today but sad tomorrow, but still maintain a high level of contentment overall (i.e. well-being). Second, one may be happy with one aspect of their life (e.g. work) but very unhappy with others (e.g. their relationships). To properly explore a person's happiness or contentment, it is vital that any measure of this should assess it across all the domains of a person's life: their relationships with family, friends and work colleagues; their work environment; their community and so on. The totality of our happiness or contentment can only be determined by exploring all domains of human existence.

What is outstanding about *The Happiness Agenda* is how it decon-
structs the concept of happiness, to unwrap its historical past, and
to try and understand why now it has become a major driver for
governments, opinion leaders and business gurus around the world.
Why is it that Gross Domestic Product is not enough for a society at
this moment in time? Did Henry David Thoreau in 1853 have some
foresight on future dilemmas in this regard when he wrote: "How
prompt we are to satisfy the hunger and thirst of our bodies; how
slow to satisfy the hunger and thirst of our souls!" This book helps
us all to truly come to terms with the worldwide phenomenon of
happiness, with all its' complexities and contradictions, putting it in
the context of contemporary life today.

Acknowledgements

The genesis, development and completion of this book have been a long and demanding journey; it was a needy, selfish and difficult thing, and could not be left alone for too long a time without engendering feelings of guilt or distraction. It has, however, been an equally rewarding as consuming an endeavour, yet required sacrifice and efforts not only by myself. So, to honour the debt owed to those who bore sufficient grace to advise, correct, challenge and suffer me throughout, my gratitude goes to: Caroline Gatrell, Colin Brown, Martin Brigham, Tim Walton and John Zoidberg; Jieyun Zhang; my family; Rob Turner and Ben Andrews; and most especially to Nik: for that which lies within is as much a testimony to you as to me.

Introduction

> [A] new measure [of] our happiness . . . could give us a general picture of whether life is improving, and that does have a really practical purpose. It will open up a national debate about what really matters; not just in government but amongst people who influence our lives: the media, in business, the people who develop the products we use, and build the towns we live in and shape the culture we enjoy.
>
> (David Cameron, 2010)

Cameron, D. (25/11/2010), on *BBC News Politics*, available at: http://www.bbc.co.uk/news/uk-11833241, accessed on 25th November, 2010.

Contemporary Anglo-American society is awash with political, organizational and individual efforts to be happy. It is extant across the realms of: governmental debates and mandates, employment policies and management consultancy advice, news stories, television fiction and documentaries, psychology, self-help courses, and even school classrooms. This widespread cultural momentum towards happiness is a culmination of events that have transpired over the past circa three hundred "Industrialized" years since the Age of Enlightenment. Throughout this period up to the modern day, happiness has come to be defined as: pursuable and attainable, able to be measured scientifically and provided by legislation, spiritual, practicable, located within the individual and attainable in correlation with the surrounding

1

capitalistic structure. Whereby a focus on one's individual, hedonistic happiness is now morally defensible, and in accordance with what have become commonly accepted societal norms. This leads to the denouement of this book that, following on from the popularized coinage of *Homo economicus* (*The Economist Online*, 2005) and even *Homo siliconvalleycus* (Thrift, 2005h: 151): modern humankind is presently aspiring toward the neologistic genus of *Homo happicus*.

The historical encroachment of this culturally defining subject position has been made manifest and is maintained by the operation and circulation of a complex, multi-levelled, multi-faceted and multi-disciplinary phenomenon, diagnosed here as the eponymous *Happiness Agenda*. The term "agenda" is employed most deliberately, for that which is transpiring is occurring simultaneously within macro-political, meso-organizational and micro-personal realms, inter- and intra-woven in and circulating between all three. Furthermore, it is an umbrella term that refers to a prevailing, generic, societal concern, which includes an array of other related "New Age" notions, such as well-being and positivity, to name but a few other comparable and even integral components; all of which are essentially focused toward the pervasive common aim of making the modern human being happy. This book is then an investigation into the legitimacy of the taken-for-granted, specifically regarding the manifest Anglo-American cultural predilection with happiness; and how, where and why the Happiness Agenda came to be so infused with our political, organizational and personal modernity.

Modern myths

> All fixed, fast frozen relations, with their train of ancient and venerable prejudices and opinions are swept away ... All that is solid melts into air, all that is holy is profaned.
>
> (Marx, [1888] 1985: 83)

In an episode from the fourth season of the HBO network's popular and critically acclaimed television drama *The Sopranos* (2002), Tony Soprano is sitting on a couch in his elderly uncle's house. The old man is sleeping, taking a brief respite from the pressures of his ongoing legal trial and battle with cancer. With Tony, and sharing staunch glasses of vodka, is Svetlana, the Russian nursemaid hired to care for the ailing, grumpy Uncle Junior, patriarch of their Mafia family. Svetlana's detached prosthetic leg is propped against an empty arm-chair and has caught Tony's eye. He appears uncharacteristically in awe of this woman, and comments quite candidly on her resilient and resolute character. With a detached and stoic nonchalance Svetlana replies, offering an incisive personal and socio-cultural commentary:

Svetlana: That's the trouble with you Americans. You expect nothing bad to ever happen when the rest of the world expect only bad to happen.
Tony: Well that's a fucking grim outlook.
Svetlana: You have everything, and still you complain. You lie on couches and bitch to your psychiatrists. You got too much time to think about yourselves.
Tony: Sounds like me alright.

This brief insight into the tribulations of a New Jersey mafioso crime syndicate provides a slightly unusual yet arguably apt and identifi-able microcosm of Anglo-American notions of being happy. For Tony Soprano is a very troubled man: his then position as "acting Boss" of his secretive fraternal cell of organized criminals causes him notable personal anxiety and distress, increasingly becoming exteriorized in numerous panic attacks and blackouts. Though it is apparently not the sinister, brutal and exploitative nature of his "work" that is the root cause of his problems (for he demonstrates limited remorse and com-passion towards victims, rivals and family-members alike—although is, a little strangely, very protective towards animals), but something acting on a deeper level. Tony is all too aware that he has money, power and a seeming free rein; often managing to elude government attempts to gather evidence for indictment against him. And yet, based on his regular therapy sessions, volatile behavior, frequent infi-delity, gorging on food, overdoses on Prozac and bouts of depression, any appreciable sense of lasting and prolonged satisfaction seems to be permanently beyond his grasp. It is thus his pervading, fundamental and active desire to *be happy*, as unsuccessful and frustrated as it may be, throughout the six seasons of the show which consumes him, and resonates with and indeed epitomizes our contemporary Zeitgeist.

George A. Miller poignantly contributes to consideration of such issues in his interrogation of what it is that "Americans around the middle of the twentieth century" tend to want and expect from life (1964: 288). His collected list of typical demands include: "We want people to like us. We do not want to be ugly ... We want money. We want to own things in which we can take pride." Other "all too familiar" expectations are: "We do not want to be fat. We do not want to smell bad. We want healthy children, and we want to be healthy ourselves." Of greatest significance though is Miller's conviction that:

> These are proven demands of the market place. Never mind whether it's good to want such things, or whether we even have a right to want them. The point is that these are the things people in America work for, spend money on, devote their lives to.
>
> (ibid.)

He describes them as being quite specifically modern, American demands, all of which have been rendered "perfectly explicit, conscious and socially acceptable." As a consequence of the sheer volume of similarly motivated individuals who crave such states of being, Miller identifies relatively few negative consequences or stigma associated with desiring good health, looks and financial security in mainstream mid-twentieth-century culture. He then asks his reader to imagine collecting a similar catalogue of typical desires from other peoples or at other times: "from Neanderthal men or the Tartar hordes." Astutely concluding that people often have trouble believing their own peculiar, established longings for popularized commodities or comportments of behavior are socially determined and "learned" rather than "universal and inevitable" (ibid.).

The fictional inner wrangling of Tony Soprano over his perpetual struggle for happiness in the scene described above forms an accord then with contemporary audiences as it is a recognizable and common lament, writ large across the structuring of modern Anglo-American society. Developing this in light of Miller's observations, the manners in which happiness is presently being sought after and provided can, and will, be deemed as having become so socially legitimate, so "explicit and acceptable," that they can be identified in formally politicized, organized and personalized practices, materializing across the activities of governments, media outlets, companies and homes. However, and of utmost importance, this strive towards *Homo happicus* should not by mere virtue of its affinity with modern humanity be confused as being an imperative, ever-present concern; in the same way that, say, consuming food and water are inescapable prerequisites of past and future existence. It has not historically always been considered such an imperative right and indeed presently is not so in many other societies. Rather it is very much "learnt," culturally and temporally specific, and predicated upon the prevalence of particular ideological developments.

In *Work and the Nature of Man* (1972), Frederick Herzberg provides valuable and interesting insights into the formation of the ideological and thematic foundations of societies. He suggests that every society must inevitably establish *myths* about themselves in order to sustain political, organizational and social institutional structures, which become necessarily elevated to the position of "societal canon" and are "willingly accepted even though patently misleading" (ibid.: 12). One possible expositional example is the concept of Manifest Destiny: a belief held by the new American colonies in the 1700 and 1800s that they were destined to expand unhindered from the Atlantic seaboard to the Pacific Ocean. More a general notion than a specific policy, it became a political catchphrase in the nineteenth century, then eventually a standardized historical term, used to justify the belief that European descendants acting as government agents had a "God-given" right to appropriate any lands, resources and native peoples (either by slaughter or internment on reservations) as was considered necessary for the establishment of the new, independent American nation (cf. Brown, 1971).

Herzberg argues that societal myths are not maintained necessarily by intellectual reasoning, but rather by the emotional support and sense of stability they can provide. To elucidate with the concept of Manifest Destiny: the Native Americans were cast as a problem to be marshalled or purged, and the colonizers as heroic figures eking out a tough living in an unforgiving landscape. Having come to the New World looking for freedom and to escape social and religious persecution, the more rapacious settlers hence provided themselves with a sense of purpose and social validation for their violent actions. This assumes that human nature is neither static nor universal, but collectively formulated within discrete pockets, reflecting "the social orders people inhabit" (Bakan, 2004: 134). Myths are thus very significant: first, in terms of the ideological support, they offer the frameworks and actions of a society; and, second, for the reciprocal, emotive attachment adherent individuals have for them. They provide a unified synergy of internal reasoning and meaning, regardless of any external logical inconsistencies they may bear, for the human agent as they navigate the world around them.

Herzberg recognized that dominant societal powers, "whether [they] be religious, political or economic," are both sustained and destroyed by the relative belief in their associated myth structures (1972: 20). For example, the early Middle Ages saw the papacy emerge victorious in a struggle for ascendancy and influence over European society, wherein it attempted to "unify all life, politically, economically and most important to control the life of the individual and of the family" (ibid.). But, as expanded upon in Chapter 2, by the sixteenth century, the power base of the Catholic Church had begun to erode, as ideologically contrasting movements awakened the belief (or *myth*) that personal achievement rather than pious, spiritual devotion was "necessary to the happiness of mankind" (ibid.: 24). Mythic revolutions and shifts in the constitution and interests of society therefore demonstrably go in unison, intimately affected by the ideas upon which they are built and the willingness—or lack thereof—of societies to continue sustaining them: "New myth systems are born when the old dogmas hurt people too much" (ibid.).

Of all the myths generated by humankind, those which are the "most far-reaching, ubiquitous and serviceable" are primarily concerned with "implicit conceptions of what people are like" (ibid.: 13). Drawing upon a number of sources, but most notably the work of Rowlands (2005), in the modern Anglo-American age, there are four such popularized myths which seem most conspicuous, epidemic and ingrained: *individualism, humanism, rationalism* and *instrumentalism*. These have all emerged, coincided and created a mythic collage which underpins the reigning, distinctive contemporary fascination with happiness. Their correlation with one another and insinuation into Anglo-American society have significantly contributed to packaging happiness as a seemingly timeless, natural and worthwhile human regard, but while the emotion of and ability to experience it are certainly innate to our species, the legion of bespoke expressions of and this socially produced preoccupation with it are not. Neither are these myths immune from succumbing to new culturally validated ideas, as despite being presently salient, they are inevitably subject to eventual usurpation.

For the purposes of this book, *individualism* is understood to be a creed that establishes the needs and desires of the human agent as central to their own activities. It is fundamentally a moral concept as it questions what sort of life it is best to live, and in the present day it seems to be one dedicated to the introspective, Maslovian principles of self-actualization, self-development and self-fulfilment. The significance of individualism is hence that self-work and self-interest are not only activities that *are* widely engaged in but ones that *should* be (cf. Rowlands, 2005: 2–5). Similarly, *humanism* is an interest in the ethical codes by which humankind consents to exist, and the "objectification of the spirit within culture and society: morality, law, state, religion, art, science and philosophy" (ibid.,: 300). It is often associated with establishing widespread parity, well-being and fairness and prioritizing human needs.

Further, *rationalism* is an epistemological position that holds there are two kinds of knowledge: that which is garnered from direct experience, and "universally valid truths concerning (for example) God, human nature and morality" (Skirbekk and Gilje, 2001: 238); both of which exist apart from individuals' entry into social relations (Townley, 2002: 556). Finally, *instrumentalism* refers to a prevailing faith in a Weberian instrumental rationality or means–ends reasoning, where the complexities of life, including valuations of subjective states, are considered reducible to units that can be evaluated in terms of a cost/benefit analysis: "in the age of modernity, everything is calculable" (ibid.: 8; cf. Cooley, 1980; Munro, 1996; Shenhav, 2003); and the world can be understood and mastered with the appropriate physical and intellectual tools.

Thus, it is under such ideological, "mythic" conditions that the individual's right to concentrate on their own happiness in a brazen and judicial way is presently considered to be justified in present Anglo-American society. In declaring that such an occurrence is "modern," it is then necessary to provide a decisive definition of the particular time period under analysis. Based on the preceding dialogue, rather than affixing restrictive, inexorable bookends to an arbitrary chronological era though, the span referred to as "modernity" is better conceived of in terms of its presiding ideologies—the bodies of doctrines, philosophies or beliefs—and their underlying, commonly shared and socially enacted concerns. Skirbekk and Gilje summate modern society as being: "the expression of an agreement between egotistical individuals dictated by everyone's common long-range and enlightened self-interest … that is acknowledged by reason" (2001: 184). "Modern" is then, in this context, a reference to the approximate historical period of the past three hundred years in which Western humankind has demanded to be reasoned, Enlightened and thereby *happy*, though calculative and political means; and during which the accession of the four prominent myths: individualism, humanism, rationalism and instrumentalism, have ascended and engendered the cultural conditions in which a generic fascination with happiness could flourish.

Pursuing happiness

> People come up to me and say: "What's wrong?" Nothing. "Well, it takes more energy to frown than it does to smile!" Yeah? You know it takes more energy to point that out than it does to leave me alone?
> (Hicks, 1992)

One archetypal exemplar of the presently heralded interpretation of happiness is a landmark document drafted and signed in 1776, by five men, including two future Presidents, declaring and uniting the then thirteen colonies of North America as independent from British rule. In addition to formally distancing the newly born country from its previous "oppressors," it set out and enshrined in law certain liberties as sacrosanct, and to be afforded to all its citizens:

> We hold these Truths to be self-evident, that all Men are created equal, that they are endowed, by their Creator, with certain unalienable Rights, that among these are Life, Liberty, and the Pursuit of Happiness.

This sentence, taken from the Declaration of Independence ratified in 1776 has come to epitomize the phantasm of the *American Dream*: the idea that through hard work and determination the opportunities of the "New World" were and are available to all. Of course the reference to "all Men" is explicitly gendered, not to mention the lack of liberty granted to those forced to endure chattel slavery, which prevailed in the southern United States for another hundred or so years. However, it is significant that the third identified right, the deliberate and active "pursuit of happiness," was being actively infused into the collective mythos of the newly allied states. While it may not then have been necessarily extended to *all* citizens in practice, its substantiation into the emerging "modern" American ideological psyche reveals a number of assumed theoretical and philosophical preconditions, congruent with the identified prominent underlying *myths* of modernity. Chiefly, that happiness is: a concept or a state to which humankind can aspire; that it is something to be pursued and is both object-like, and elusive, requiring capture; and those seeking it must take self-responsible, proactive and decisive steps towards securing it.

This particular definitional construction of happiness has certainly not always been so prevalent. In earlier epochs it has been associated with the notions of chance, fortune, silliness, wealth, blitheness and even being wise. Duncan enounces though that in the past three or so centuries: "happiness has acquired a private, subjective meaning, largely to do with good feelings" (2007: 87). What becomes paramount then is to establish why such a change in the widely accepted definition and elevation in the societal importance of happiness has occurred, and thus how the subject position of *Homo happicus* came to be such a fundamental aspiration for so many Anglo-American politicians, organizations and individuals.

Richard Dawkins, Oxford University's Charles Simonyi Professor for the Public Understanding of Science, addresses how one might attempt to discuss the prolific, diffuse and even byzantine manner in which such movements emerge and gain momentum, and replace previously dominant hegemonies:

> We need to explain why the changing moral Zeitgeist is so widely synchronized across large numbers of people; and we need to explain its relatively consistent direction. It spreads itself from mind to mind through conversations in bars and at dinner parties, through books and book reviews, through newspapers and broadcasting, and nowadays through the Internet. Changes in the moral climate are signalled in editorials, on radio talk shows, in political speeches, in the patter of stand-up comedians and the scripts of soap operas, in the votes of parliaments making laws and the decisions of judges interpreting them.
>
> (2006: 270)

It will therefore be postulated herein that three principal epiphe-nomenal events described as *shocks*, founded upon the ideological myths that sustain modern society, have occurred in the past three hundred years since the Age of Enlightenment. These have been trig-gers which expedited the contemporary combined political, organi-zational and personal enchantment with happiness. These shocks are, respectively: (1) the nineteenth-century Utilitarian rendering of happiness from a philosophical to a macro-political concept; (2) its subsequent twentieth-century operationalization into meso-organizational activity and Human Relations thinking; and (3) the twenty-first-century emergence of "positivity" theories in renowned micro-individual social psychologies.

The word "shock" is not then an inference in any way of a sense of immediacy. It rather designates the advancement of intellectual and cultural evolutions, not an unexpected event transpiring at great speed. That which is shocking is the eventual results, their compat-ibilities and the ideological transformations of anxieties from one historical epoch to another, not the expediency of their ascent. The shocks are three events which have greatly influenced the cultural circulation and acceptance of happiness as a modern concern. They are not deemed to be the sole generators, but rather those that seem most identifiable across the three macro-, meso- and micro-realms of society. Significantly, each is validated by and acts to influence the other two, providing a tripartite, society-encompassing system of internal consistency and logic. That dramatically influences the present understanding of happiness regarding what are morally viable definitions and actions for governments, companies and citizens.

From the onset, however, there are a host of complications in attempting to write about concepts, movements and phenomena in society that trade with and in such emotive and subjective notions. First, happiness, well-being, positivity (and other similar terms), could each arguably warrant numerous books in their own right and, while certainly connected, can be analyzed from a number of perspectives and as separate and discrete entities. Further, there is no one single, identifiable group of academics or practitioners publishing, investigat-ing and promoting these subjects—in fact quite the opposite, as disci-plines as diverse as sociology, biology, psychology, economics, politics and religious studies are all increasingly focusing on them—and no clearly labelled shelf in a library which a motivated researcher could simply spend their days diligently ploughing through.

Finally, and adding most notably to the complexity of this potential quagmire, to attempt to provide a "critical" assessment or redress of such a paradigm is to also potentially open oneself quite vulnerably to various antonymic labels: negative, pessimist, defeatist, cynic; all could seem quite apt of an argument, and its author, that stutters and fidgets somewhat at the often perfunctory talk, thought and practice towards fervently engineering, enabling and empowering happy and positive people. The tautological desire and naturalized right to want and be happy is so pervasive at the entwining politico-philosophical, organizational and personal levels of modern life that to refuse, resist or even question an active, "positive interest in people's happiness" is often considered to be wrong, aberrant or bizarre behavior (cf. Duncan, 2007: 86). This is because the "pursuit of happiness" is such a constituent part of the accepted common-sense mythos and cultural backdrop of today, that virtually any criticism is thereby cast automatically as an opposing and denigrating countervailing to the mainstream.

The aim of this book is then not to produce some innovative formula for how happiness can be benchmarked or cultivated, but neither to merely "snipe from the sidelines" (cf. Parker, 2002) at other efforts to do so. There is certainly great benefit to be found by facilitating workspaces and populations that are conducive to promoting happier lives for those who use and form part of them. The discussion here endeavors rather to expose the underlying similarities in approach of certain influential paradigms of thought that have aligned to produce a characteristic conception of how people should best "be," and why these have been so actively and widely embraced. Instead of following the trend of so many "how-to" publications offering prescriptive techniques to find, measure and increase happiness, that provided here is then an original explanation as to *why* such offers and efforts are presently so seductive.

The (social) science of happiness

Any act of social research is inherently purposive, as the collation, examination and ascription of meaning to data necessarily involve an attempt to engineer change: "Change in the researcher, change in the researched, change in the user of the research" (Clough and

Nutbrown, 2002: 12). In addition to the necessity of effecting a change, Clough and Nutbrown demand that any "research is ... a moral act" and as such: "the researcher holds responsibility for ensuring that resulting change is ... for the social good" (ibid.: 4). The primary "change" aspired to here is thus to highlight how a major accepted narrative of the modern day, the sustained imperative to make oneself and others happy, as bemoaned by Bill Hicks (1992), is an ideological and social conspiracy-of-coordination between certain powerful ideas, institutions and actors. What is so all-pervading in Anglo-American social reality is effectively concealed by the very fabric of its constitution, but which will hopefully now be rendered amenable to discussion, enabling an understanding of why we are so wrapped up in our cultural preoccupations, rather than just accepting and re-producing them. This is in order to "identify the cracks in this new [secular] religion" (Parker, 2002: 9), as happiness has, in certain ways, become as though a faith: with political, corporate and social institutions acting as churches, certain advocates and gurus as ministers, and, vitally, one's self the god.

The current obsession with happiness will thus be revealed ultimately as being akin to a *Potemkin Village*: that which appears sound, habitable and defensible but is rather a produced façade. It must be reiterated that this is not a calculated defilement of the notion of happiness, the right to be happy, or attempts to build and measure systems to promote it, as the word "façade," and indeed "conspiracy," are here used to refer to the social production of interest in happiness in the present epoch—thereby making it something very *real* in terms of its effects. It is not being stated that happiness or attempts to be happy are in any way fake but, again, rather that this interest in happiness is temporally and culturally "learned" (recall Miller, 1964: 289) and will eventually shift. The term "Potemkin Village" is often used in dissenting from a residing majority opinion when it is felt that which is commonly held or espoused is not indubitably an accurate depiction of an event or circumstance. As a simile, then, it helps emphasize why and how we are so preoccupied with happiness, rather than simply maintaining that it is both natural to be so and that we, timelessly, always have, will and should be.

Based on the above predicates, the circulation of happiness evident today is: widespread, meta-structural, ideological and practical; and is hence described anon as a *mass-discursive, cultural phenomenon*. It is a disciplinary mechanism that operates through people, technologies and ideas, forming a fragmented but coordinated preoccupation that permeates and circulates throughout, to some degree, virtually all levels of Anglo-American society. It provides an appealing subject position, designated here as *Homo happicus*, to aspire toward, by justifying and enabling the pursuit of one's own happiness across political, organizational and personal spectrums of society, supported by the salience of individualist, humanist, rationalist and instrumentalist myths. It is, however, vital to state that this "Happiness Agenda" is not an all-controlling system minutely dictating human action. As revealed in the following chapters, it is rather a framework of disparate but foundationally connected activity, which essentially relies upon human appropriation and interpretation for its continued existence.

To examine this phenomenon in detail, the next four chapters of this book establish a theoretical model for *the cultural circuits of happiness*; determining initially in Chapter 1 the intellectual architecture to be embraced throughout. In this chapter, Professor Nigel Thrift's myriad discussions of the spread and translations of "new capitalism" (Thrift, 2005a) across the globe are explicated, utilized and restructured into a format that enables the conceptualization and interrogation of the prolific spread of happiness. They are augmented with a number of additional, congruous theories, providing an intellectual pathway with which to explore a contingent and rhizomatic historical network of events, myths, theories, objects and practices, that were not ineluctable but rather transpired as a result of the congruencies between different dominant groups and ideas, each with a vested interest in happiness.

Chapters 2, 3, and 4 then each respectively consider the three macro-, meso- and micro-realm ideological shocks that have generated and propelled the modern obsession with happiness. To repeat, these are: (1) the utilitarian rendering of happiness from a philosophical to a political concept; (2) its operationalization in human relations thinking and organizational activity; and (3) its "positive" emergence and embrace in renowned individual centric social-psychological disciplines. Chapter 5 summarizes the preceding analyses of this agenda, and highlights the "spiritual" facet of its modern embrace. Chapter 6 then investigates the manner in which it is necessarily "appropriated," and finally Chapter 7 offers some projections of its possible future.

This work hence contributes to a wide array of managerial, philosophical and sociological literature, as the subject matter is itself composed, and so the relative depths and purposes of the interrogations herein differ and the overall approach cannot be said to be exclusively aimed at any one discipline. This is justifiable, however, as:

> Causation in history is a tricky problem, never simple ... Material, social and intellectual factors continually interact on each other. It is not clear that they do so within the matrix of a single system, so that one can speak of the unity of an historical epoch. Any historical period contains within itself many processes and themes, not necessarily all knit together in a seamless web; there are always loose ends.
>
> (Stromberg, 1981: 12)

The cultural impetus to be happy is thereby presented as is indicative of its nature: complex, unconventional and varying in focus and direction. Having above referenced the Anglo-American right to strive for happiness as apotheosized in the Declaration of Independence, this book offers a novel interpretation, investigation and effort to understand the strivings of the Happiness Agenda, and the history, structure and champions of a modern obsession.

1
The happy adventures of capital

> Thoughts survive if they work, if they propagate, if
> they find an appropriate milieu, a welcoming terri-
> tory . . . There are thoughts that repeat themselves
> over and over again, positioning themselves as
> unquestionable obstacles. There are thoughts that
> attempt to ground themselves in other success-
> ful thoughts and bring an affective reward. There
> are thoughts that organise human life so success-
> fully that they manifest their own truth in their
> performance.
>
> (Goodchild, 1996: 211 cited in Thrift, 1999: 31)

In order to form a valid assessment of the manner and extent to
which happiness has emerged as a conspicuous *lingua franca* in
present Anglo-American society, a robust philosophical framework
must first be established. This chapter presents an interrogation and
expansion of existing correlative theoretical perspectives, which,
when conjoined, enable the analysis of the spread and dynamics of
such mass-discursive, cultural phenomena. These academic anteces-
sors include actor-network, rhizomatic and Foucauldian theories and,
as their principal structure and expositional exemplar, Thrift's seminal
body of work on the global cultural circulation of capital (2005a).

In the first section, a preliminary overview of Thrift's understanding of the *circuits* of "new" capitalism is provided, in order to intro-
duce its intricate and sophisticated nature, and theoretical similarity
with the contemporary Anglo-American endeavor to be happy. The

following two sections then expand upon the issues raised: with the first specifically detailing how capitalism, being used as a demonstrative test-case for the Happiness Agenda, is both *reflexive* and *complex*, and the prominent agents and manners by which it acts; and the second addressing the integral roles of objects and subjects. The next section then considers the problems that are inherent to the economic system's current embodiment; and the final section correlates this novel theoretical view of capitalism, or of mass-discursive, cultural phenomena in general, directly to the neoteric study of the modern emergence and proliferation of happiness.

The culture of capital: an overview

> Capitalism in all its brutality was stalking the land, convincing of its liberating role those who wished to be convinced.
>
> (Hill, 1996: 40 cited in Scott, 1998: 119)

The above quote from the British Marxist historian Christopher Hill concerning the affective and coursing nature of capital was written in reference to the closing years of the seventeenth century. It denotes a system wrought with forceful influence, able to insinuate itself into the very essence of the social world. While written in an admonitory tone, it however also arguably relates to analysis of the contemporary "new" capitalist system (Scott, 1998: 119).

Having written on the phenomenon in great detail, in 2005, Thrift published a collection of his works detailing modern capitalism, much like happiness, as an holistic, circulatory world-scale entity. Entitled *Knowing Capitalism* (2005a), his book provides an anthology with which to make sense of the political and economic world around us. He explicitly states that "something new" is currently happening to contemporary Western capitalism: "For so the story goes, firms now live in a permanent state of emergency, always bordering on the edge of chaos" (Thrift, 2005h: 130). Rather than more traditional, industrial-era models of bureaucratic control, "new" capital is defined by the implementation of "managerialist" (Parker, 2002) practices, such as: project work, teams, flattened hierarchies, and knowledge workers, with the capacity to "change" and "hair trigger responsiveness" deemed key to organizational survival (Thrift, 2005h:130).

In addition to this plethora of novel practices, that which is explicitly "new" about contemporary capitalism is its cultural migration
into the "symbolic realm," where it has become something now "so
self-evident," it is simultaneously "both everywhere and nowhere"
(Thrift, 2005c: 20). This is referred to generically as *the rise of soft
capitalism* (cf. Heelas, 2002), whereby a collective, societal "act of
amnesia" has occurred, enabling the effects and mechanisms of capital to become so engrained in the modern epoch that they are "more
difficult to see" (Thrift, 2005c: 20). Reminiscent of Miller's (1964: 288)
insights and the introductory discussion of happiness above, capitalism is hence often deemed to be both timeless and natural. This has
occurred due to a series of ideological and sociological developments,
or *shocks*. Namely, the increasing stress on subjectivity and self, the
growth of information technologies and their associated new possibilities of learning and knowledge; and the rise of new forms of
theory, which stress "decentredness, multiple times and spaces, and
the discursive realm" (ibid.: 20–1). Enabling the declaration that:
"Somehow, human life (in the West at least) ha[s] transited into a
distinctive historical space where everything was different and, well,
modern" (ibid.: 27).

So, while a more classic approach to political economy may "still
have a lot of life left in it" (Thrift, 2001: 375), it is unlikely that more
nuanced understanding of the present will come from well-trodden,
narrow emphases on "money and finance" or "information technology" (Thrift, 2005b: 5). Focus should rather be on the cultural
dimension of such world-scale phenomena, and the driving power of
their circulation, as cultural impulses, like "new capitalism" and the
Happiness Agenda, thrive and spread upon "extraordinary discursive
apparatus" (Thrift, 2001: 377). Rather than being merely a gathering
of, say, abstract economic or philosophical theorems, they are an
emergent and patchwork product of modern institutional, technological and psychological reality.

This process of cultural circulation operates via foundational "series
of relations" (Thrift, 2005b: 17). The first of which is the embodiment
of processes by human patrons, or *actors*: "which assume that this is
how the world is ... written into the body and other spatial layouts
through repetition" (ibid.: 2). In specific reference to "new" capitalism: governments, the media, companies and individuals (all of
whom can be considered actors) regard one another participating in

and with the dynamics of capitalism and thereby engage in it them-selves. This is reminiscent of institutionalist discussions of mimeti-cism: the "tendency of organizations to copy the forms adopted by [others]" (Ackroyd, 2002: 246). In both contexts, those involved reproduce, reinforce and catalyze the similar relational and structural ways of being and doing commonly expounded and institutionalize them, establishing: "a set of practices that are customary or habitual, and have come to exist over a long period of time" (ibid.: 193).

Significantly, mimetic modes of both organization and capitalism are not necessarily repeated exactly or in their entirety, but rather in relation to localized politically and culturally distinct niches, producing variant strains at provincial and international levels, yet all remaining sufficiently recognizable as parts of the whole: "Institutions typically endure: they persist in roughly the same configuration, changing gradually over time" (ibid.). For example, Hutton (2002) and Gray (2002) both discuss the variances between British, continental European, North American, Russian and Asian "strains" of capitalism—all of which perform with marked differ-ences, but interact with, influence and strengthen the validity of one another. Thus, actors engage in the capitalist process, albeit with culturally characteristic variations, and by occurring it becomes repeated and validated, leading to yet further occurrences.

The second generalized series of relations by which mass-discursive, cultural phenomena operate is through the production and interven-tions of non-human *objects* (Thrift, 2005b: 2). The term "object" – also described as "cultural products" (ibid.) or "weapons" (Thrift, 2005h: 137) – is potentially representative of much. In relation to capital it can refer to: "delivery schedules to barcodes to office layouts to charts," and social structures as much as to physical items. Acting in a similar capacity to actors, objects "assume the world is actively medi-ated in particular ways and directs bodies along these ways" (ibid.). The objects produced as consequence of these large-scale cultural sys-tems – such as books or seminars about either managerialist business techniques or how to become happier – hence act to represent and rein-force the social environment and actors which led to their creation.

The final general series of relations concerns behavior-influencing *templates*: "that, instituted as practices, roll over particular ways of doing people [actors] and things [objects]" (Thrift, 2005c: 2). Intimately connected with the previous two, this relates to how "subject positions" are formulated by corporate, political and societal institutions, whereby acceptable ways of being and relative social morality are all produced, disseminated and internalized in the human arena. As above, such processes occur and are then witnessed and repeated, eventually leading to their manifest legitimacy. Importantly, within such processes humankind is not labelled as unwitting, cultural dupes, brainwashed into accepting a predetermined vision of the world. They are rather surrounded by a mass-discursive, cultural phenomenon's complicated and seductive system of actors, objects and behavioral templates, which are themselves determined by how human agents actively choose to interact with them.

In light of this introduction to these series of relations by which such systems function, Thrift discriminates quite clearly how they should be studied. First, with clear echoes of Foucauldian thinking, one should adopt a "backward gaze," acting as an historian of the future might while pondering back upon today. This is to limit sweeping claims that may "set the seal on history," and ensure we understand the contemporary as a temporally and culturally peculiar snapshot along a continuum fraught with unresolved issues, differences in interpretation and agents and actions very much in motion (ibid.: 2; Thrift, 2001: 376), providing a *history of the present* (cf. Foucault, 1991: 31).

Second is the assertion that historical events "have a good deal of contingency built into them" (Thrift, 2005b: 3). The passage of history was not an inevitable path, nor one of necessarily clear, progressive improvement from which we can say the ideas of today are superior to those of yesterday based solely on their more recent genesis. It is also counter-productive to search for discrete and definitive triggers that will explain in absolute terms why the modern world is as it appears. Rather a *rhizomatic* (cf. Deleuze and Guattari, 1988) perspective seems more appropriate whereby the course of events are seen as developing from a multiplicity of influences.

Third, as postulated above, Thrift iterates that these efforts are "performative," or a perpetually unfinished project (2001: 376). For example, influential firms and nations may "do their best to steer [capitalism] in certain directions," but emergent energy crises, protests or financial downturns (for example) can render both political and corporate institutions as having to ever-find "a new set of responses to a new set of problems" (ibid.). This perma-lack of completion is created by the highly adaptive, expansive and constantly mutating nature of mass-discursive, cultural phenomena, and any analysis must reflect and allow for this.

The fourth and final rule identified is: "always look for the routine, even boring, as well as the sexy" (Thrift, 2005b: 3). In relation again to capital, despite the necessary ability to adapt and evolve, it functions essentially by maintaining core customs and assumptions. In addition to the obligatory functional processes of the systematic exploitation of surplus value and reciprocal exchange, these are argued here to presently include the systemic maintenance of the myths of: individualism, humanism, rationalism and instrumentalism. Four themes which very much influence the present organization and governance (not to mention the desire to be happy) in contemporary Anglo-American society, and also inform the minutiae of personal, social and business interactions.

Returning then to the Marxian overtones in the above opening quote, Thrift is clear in locating his conceptualization of "new" capitalism as distinct from such dystopian descriptions that render it merely as a system of oppression that "deadens" what it touches. Considering it alternatively as embodying an "unholy, crazy vitality" that can "possess but also create" (ibid.: 17), stating with resonance that it is not just "hard graft" but "also fun" (ibid.: 1):

> Many of those working in the *new economy* wanted to believe in more-than business. For them, the new economy isn't primarily a financial institution. Like painting and sculpting, business can be a venue for personal expression and artistry. At its heart it is more like a canvas than a spreadsheet.
>
> (Thrift, 2005g: 121, emphasis in original)

Neither modern capitalism nor the Happiness Agenda are then akin to Hill's seventeenth-century representation of a thuggish con-artist, nor merely symptomatic of an ever-encroaching systemic influence of formal rationality into human life: "I have no truck with accounts of capitalism that insist [it] has disenchanted the world" (Thrift, 2005ba: 2). Their cultural prominence and proliferation though, as astutely observed by Hill (1996: 40) and recalling Herzberg (1972), are inescapably contingent upon the nature and tenacity by which they are embraced and operated by willing actors, and embodied by their associated objects and templates. This introductory analysis thus presents mass-discursive, cultural phenomena as intricate and complex cultural systems, the detailed dynamics of which can now be further examined.

A reflexive complexity

> [A]lmost blind and mute, even though it makes others see and speak.
> (Deleuze, 1986: 35, cited in Thrift, 2005b: 1)

Having outlined the general tenets of the cultural dynamics of "new" capitalism, it is now possible to expand further upon a number of the integral issues, in order to explicate how such phenomenon become insinuated within modernity. In the very opening line of *Knowing Capitalism*, Thrift describes his book as being about: "what happened when capitalism began to consider its own practices on a continuous basis" (2005b: 1), establishing immediately a discussion of a complex arrangement of processes, theories, beliefs, actions and structures that collaborate to form an ideology, which is reflexive enough to be both aware of itself and able to reflect inwardly upon its own machinations. This is not, however, an anthropomorphic assertion that such mass-discursive, cultural phenomena are sentient entities, capable of a Cartesian "I think, therefore I am" pronouncement. Neither are they the result of deliberately coordinated and orchestrated plans determined by a controlling group of individuals or organizations with specific intentions. As Thrift maintains: "I am not at all convinced that the managers of capitalist firms – jointly or severally – know what they are doing for quite a lot of the time" (ibid.: 2).

Despite abundant examples throughout modern history of the Anglo-American economic powers encouraging, through the offer of trade, relief or military force, other sovereign states to adopt variations of capitalism, the discussion of it in this and Thrift's book is not sympathetic to any form of grand conspiracy theory. Capitalism is not being intimately and minutely governed by an all-knowing and powerful elite, being forced to play out according to some covert, politically orchestrated Machiavellian scheme. Rather, it is a constructed, concerted effort that is coordinated specifically in the existence of the numerous economic transactions, philosophical theories, and political policies concerned with it. That, when considered in their entirety on a global scale, can be conceived of as a single "thing," with a relatively uniform direction, composed collectively of its myriad, disparate effects.

A plague of locusts is comprised of a gigantic number of individual entities which act in relative unison and collaboration, but the plague itself, as an abstracted noun, is not alive or acting at the behest of any one insect. However, to watch it devour field after field of crops or in flight through the air, it could understandably be considered as a "living" beast in its own right, and even as having malign intentions. Only in this sense is capitalism an entity in and of itself, and capable of reflexivity. For to engage with, partake in or even merely to consider capitalism, as an individual, organization or political institution, is to be a part of it, thereby rendering it a system that can be described as self-aware, based on the sentience of – some of – its individual constituent actors. It is hence an "impulse without determined goals ... instantiated in particular processes" (ibid.: 1), that informs, favors, promotes, underlies and inculcates certain modes of behavior and theoretical perspectives that have currently achieved popularity in influential circles. As consequence, "new" capitalism can be conceived as:

> A continual struggle to release new forms of representation that can capture how the world is, new forms of subject that can populate the world, new forms of commodity that can hold the world in their grip, and new forms of surface that can define how space and time should turn up in that world.
>
> (ibid.: 13)

This quote aptly reflects Thrift's three series of relations, and four methodological rules, and further affirms the essentially cultural – rather than merely financial or technological – manner in which these phenomena operate.

Thus, with a discussion of modern capitalism being by necessity one of culture, the contemporary guise of this "new" economic system is understandable, to a significant degree, as being discursive (cf. Thrift, 2001: 377). Discourse is a tricky word though perhaps too often bandied around or shied away from, but, using the following definition, is arguably appropriate when discussing the operation of the circulation of influential cultural constructs:

> Discourses are metalanguages that instruct people how to live as people. They are best represented as great rivers of communication,

performances propelled into movement by talk and text, enflamed by technologies like books, visual images, and other "media", guided by procedures like rules and styles, and crowned by significant effects like particular subject positions or emotional states which establish the cultural performance of a discourse at gut level, and allow it to kick in.

(Thrift, 2005c: 24)

In the above quote, "discourses" can effectively be replaced with "capitalism." This is not to assert that capitalism is entirely reducible to discourse, but rather to establish how its "new" forms of knowledge circulate throughout society. Furthermore, it echoes the preceding quote from Thrift directly above and is reminiscent of Dawkins' earlier cited discussion of how to track a "changing moral zeitgeist" (2006: 270). Corroborating the argument that "new" capital has "migrated" to a discursive, cultural cohort of: images, theories and interactions; fueled by: myths, technologies, texts and rules—providing participants with a morally desirable template or "way of being."

Some of the major "producers of knowledge" (Thrift, 1999: 42) that have promulgated this "new" capitalist discourse, particularly since the post-1960s period (cf. Boltanski and Chiapello, 2005: 114), are the institutions of: management schools, consultants and gurus (Thrift, 2005b: 6; 2005f: 95; 2005g: 114). Expanding upon the first set of relations by which mass-discursive, cultural phenomenon operate, these three agents, or "actors" (Thrift, 2005b: 2), are individually and collectively primarily "responsible for capitalism's spread across the globe," and, therefore, are essentially "as important" as the ideas being transmitted themselves (Thrift, 2005c: 34). While they are certainly not the only players involved, they are some of the most consequential as they generate much of the "new" capitalist, managerialist knowledge upon which other kindred actors, objects and templates circulate and are validated. Thrift also refers, although to a much lesser degree, to the role of the media in this process as being "key means of transport, amplifiers, and generators" of this knowledge (2005f: 96). Identifying specifically *The Financial Times* – which even referred to itself as *the* "newspaper of the new economy" (Thrift, 2005g: 114) – and more generally a "vast range" of other media outlets, as manifest encouragements to the three core institutions to "sing" (2005c: 54).

Learning "new" capitalism

To explicate upon this main tripartite process of "new" capitalist circulation: the increasingly formalized provision of *management education*, in particular the master of business administration (MBA) course, has proliferated the number of academics and students who produce, transmit and internalize "new" ideas of capitalism (Thrift, 2005c: 34–5; 2005f: 96). The North American model of the business school in particular has grown exponentially since its inception and been exported throughout the world as the "inter-face" of conjoined cultural and economic progression (Starkey and Tempest, 2005: 62). The concept of management education is detailed by Currie and Knights (2003: 28) as having begun at the West Point military academy and as increasing in demand and provision with the development and rapid expansion of the Pennsylvania railroad corporation in the middle of the nineteenth century. The first business school, Wharton, was established soon after in 1881 "in response to industrialization and the need for train-ing managers" (ibid.), and of the other most prestigious subsequent schools, Harvard was founded in 1908 and Stanford in 1925. Similar moves later occurred in the United Kingdom, with the simulacrum creations of the London and Manchester Business Schools in the 1960s.

They have since grown and spread at a faster rate than any other university departments (Starkey *et al.*, 2004: 1521) taking their "new" knowledge with them. As demonstrated by the fact that in the United States almost one quarter of all college students major in a business course while, accordingly, the number of management schools has increased circa 500 per cent since the mid-1950s (Thrift, 1999: 43; 2005c: 35): "They now form the most visible tips of a vast global busi-ness education iceberg, one that turns over billions of dollars per year" (Thrift, 2005f: 96). The MBA has hence emerged "as the only global degree," as its model of Western capitalistic education has become relatively homogeneous worldwide (Starkey *et al.*, 2004: 1521; cf. Pfeffer and Fong, 2004: 1501). Despite its popularity though, the MBA is reported as not necessarily correlating directly with career success (Starkey and Tempest, 2005: 63), and has been criticized for its "weird, almost unimaginable design" and for: "creating only narrowly focused graduates, 'critters with lopsided brains, icy hearts, and shrunken souls'" (Leavitt, 1989: 39, cited in Starkey and Tempest, 2005: 64).

Doing "new" capitalism

Continuing the circuits of "new" capital, much of this academic "business knowledge" is imbibed and (re)distributed by *management consultants*, who "package" these ideas: "usually producing formulas which can be applied over and over again in different situations" (Thrift, 2005c: 36). These companies have also undergone a radical expansion since the 1960s, whereby ten years later in the 1970s their collective reported revenue had doubled (ibid.: 35), and in the 1980s the industry was the "fastest growing of many advanced economies … 80% of firms currently in the industry were established after 1980" (Fincham and Clark, 2002: 3). By the end of the 1970s, world-wide revenue for the management advice industry was estimated at approximately $3 billion; by 1999, this figure was valued at around $60 billion.

It is not sufficient to assume that demand for management consultants and education increased either axiomatically or independently from one another, as their growths were mutually beneficial with each contributing to the creation and maintenance of a cultural-economic climate amenable to the other. Fusaro and Miller thus expand upon the relationship between the two institutions:

> The other main career choice for the MBA (after quick-start "dot. com" companies) has been management consultancy. Management consultancies and business school professors played a significant role in lauding the pioneering new management practices of firms such as Enron. Indeed, one of Enron's most praised management practices, before its fall from grace, was the recruitment of top MBAs from the elite business schools.
> (Fusaro and Miller, 2002, cited in Starkey and Tempest, 2005: 65)

This situation was compounded by a notable cultural shift in this era in the image of management from that of *savior* to that of *problem* (Parker, 2002: 9). As indicated above, a common feature of a number of consultancies is the claim to offer their remedying services in an attractive, functional and simplistic package: "to meet the competitive requirements for the times" (Fincham and Clark, 2002: 1). Jackson enquires then with targeted interest: "What is it about *this* time and place that has created such an extraordinary demand for management [education]?" (2003: 3, emphasis added).

In response, a number of academics and journalist-cum-commentators on global political-economy (such as Hutton, 1996; 2002, and Wheen, 2004) propose a definitive watershed in recent Anglo-American history that instigated influential political, economic and social changes that contributed significantly to the emergence of "new" capitalism. Friday, 3 May 1979, saw the election of a new Conservative Government and first female Prime Minister in Britain, Margaret Thatcher, by the largest voter margin of victory since 1966. It was this change in Parliament that catalyzed a dramatically enhanced cultural interest in "new" capitalist and managerialist knowledge (Furusten, 1999: 1). From her ascension to power, Thatcher was an avid aficionado and harbinger of the "New Right's" beliefs in the ultimate economic supremacy of markets, competition and individualism (Hutton, 1996). The prior dominance of Keynesian economics was aggressively rejected (Rose, 2004; Galbraith, 1996: 31), as Thatcher, along with the contemporaneous President of the United States, Ronald Reagan, jointly heralded the withdrawal of direct state support of commercially viable organizations (Owen, 1999: 3; Hutton, 2002), promoting deregulation, privatization and the marked reduction of state social provision (Hutton, 1996: 169).

The syzygy between the government and consultancies, fueled by their joint fascination with managerialist ideas, goes even further. From the 1960s management consultants had been employed by the British government, but during the 1980s, in harmony with their rising status in the business world, this dramatically increased as governmental agencies attempted to render their administration "more business-like" in accordance with their new economic mantras (Saint-Martin, 2000: 3). This led to radical alterations within governmental and corporate organizations well into the 1990s. Rigid, centralized and hierarchical forms of bureaucracy were lambasted as grossly inefficient (ibid.: 1) and much greater emphasis was placed on the roles and actions of managers as the dynamic drivers of change and improvement (Furusten, 1999: 149–50). As to how to institutionalize such streamlined, restructured and smooth-running functioning, consultants were, understandably, more than "willing to explain, for a fee, just how this could be achieved" (Wheen, 2004: 39).

Recalling mass-discursive, cultural phenomena's integral series of relations, the frequent repetition, employment and utilization of management education and consultancy ideas by the Anglo-American states had a dual effect. First, it was mutually beneficial for both Thatcher's and Reagan's "*neo*-liberal" governments, as advice from the private and academic sectors lent a sense of rationality and legitimacy to their treasured conservative economic policies, with which they redesigned state, public and commercial relations. This effectively reconstituted the notions of government and citizenry, with individuals becoming redefined as "clients" able to make choices in a "market-like" fashion (Saint-Martin, 2000: 1). Society and the economy were therefore rendered as more amenable to "arm's length" governance (Greer, 1994: 2), as a diversity of actors effectively self-regulated in accordance with the managerialist behavioral templates of competition and efficiency.

Second, management consultants and educators on either side of the Atlantic equally secured the growth and validity of their professions, helping them to make claims to positions of supreme authority based on their now-perceived government-endorsed specialist and practicable expertise (cf. Miller and O'Leary, 1989). They were hence enabled, holistically, to recommend forms of state intervention, business action and market conditions that best suited their own deeply vested interests and ensured repeat custom (Greer, 1994: 29). This cultural propagation of "new" capitalist ideas with firmly established experts and champions, referred to as the emergence of a *Consultocracy* (Saint-Martin, 2000: 20), resulted in their influencing of "human life so successfully that they manifest their own truth in their performance" (recall Goodchild, 1996: 211, cited in Thrift, 1999: 31).

The appeal to governments of this discourse on economic and state governance was thus understandably strong. Sklair, reminiscent of Hill (1996: 40), even reports that the self-justifying rhetoric it produces is "designed to persuade" people that the system is "natural, fair and fundamentally better than any realistic alternative" (1995: 98–9). Such a politico-economic environment, combined with the dramatic growth of the consulting and management education industries, resulted in an ideological *conspiracy-of-coordination*, able to spread further than ever before the agenda of "new" capitalism, resulting in what was described by Fukuyama (1992) as the "end point" of mankind's ideological evolution:

The demise of the Marxist states in Eastern Europe seemed to vindicate all that [Thatcher] and Reagan had done: both socialism and Keynesianism had been pronounced dead, and unrestrained turbo-capitalism installed as the new orthodoxy.

(Wheen, 2004: 39)

It is of importance to note here that the British Tory Government was usurped by Blair's New Labour Party in the 1997 general election. Many commentators hence thought a decisive change would occur with the repeal of neo-liberal and privatization policies (cf. Hutton, 1996). There were, however, many clear correlations between New Labour and Thatcher's (and subsequently Major's) conservatism, as Blair effectively realigned his loyalties away from his party's trade union background: "Both Tony Blair and Gordon Brown have come to believe that there is enough that is correct about the conservative propositions to make it unnecessary to challenge them" (Hutton, 2002: 229). Notably, both Blair and Brown maintained a strong advocacy of "new" managerialist economic policies, enhancing their already profound cultural, and world-wide, economic dominance. Likewise, they have arguably been similarly maintained by the Tory-Liberal Democrat coalition government ushered into power on 6 May 2010. As an aside, perhaps there is then a cosmic irony at play in the moniker of "Tony Blair, PM" producing the unfortunate anagram "I'm Tory Plan B."

Teaching "new" capitalism

The final prominent agent in the circuits of capital is the *management guru*. This corps includes various types: academics like Michael Porter and Gareth Morgan; consultants like James Champy and Peter Drucker; and hero-managers like Donald Trump and Lord Alan Sugar (cf. Thrift, 2005c: 36). There is also an echelon of *a*typical gurus, like Benjamin Zander, conductor of the Boston Philharmonic, who provides lectures on music as a metaphor for management (ibid.). Further, there are available an almost endless supply of biographic management advice books, that posthumously apply the actions of famous historical figures to contemporary organizational problems. Aside from the not infrequent, popularized allusions to Machiavelli and Sun Tzu, some of the more peculiar include: *The Wisdom of Alexander the Great: Enduring Leadership Lessons from the Man Who Created an Empire* (Kurke, 2004); *A Higher Standard of Leadership: Lessons from the Life of Gandhi* (Nair, 1997); and *The Management Methods of Jesus: Ancient Wisdom for Modern Business* (Briner, 2001).

Fincham and Clark state that, much like consultants, management gurus in their varying capacities are so pervasive that: "few people, whether in their roles as employees or as citizens, will have avoided their effects altogether" (2002: 1). Another author who has investigated this literature in great depth is the afore-cited Jackson, who speaks to his own experiences of being a "young manager" looking to publications that "made [him] feel emotionally good about what [he] was doing" and were littered with references to "enthusiasm" and "tremendous fun" (2003: 1). He suggests that his desires for validity were often replaced by the presentation style, support for and persona of the author, creating a parallel with Thrift's earlier cited identification of capitalism being for many people not just "hard graft" but "also fun" (2005b: 1).

The available supply of personalities who trade as gurus in and transmit managerialist ideas is in great abundance and as such would be impossible to analyse in their entirety. Certain prominent examples can, however, be identified and seen as "significant spokespersons for the general discourse" (Furusten, 1999: 13). In addition to publishing a quarterly review regularly send out to prominent clients, the major American consultancy firm McKinsey commissioned the production of 54 books (cf. *The McKinsey Way*, Rasiel, 2000) between 1980 and 2004, correlating with the chronological advance of management education and the New Right's political embracement of consulting companies. The most famous of these is probably *In Search of Excellence* (1982) by two of their then employees, Tom Peters and Robert Waterman – both of whom hold doctorates and have long acted as consultants for McKinsey and as "lone star" gurus (Furusten, 1999: 76).

Furusten describes *In Search of Excellence* as "relentlessly optimistic" and designed to say the right thing at the right time (ibid.: 5). Fortuitously, it was published in the very week when US unemployment had reached its apex since the Depression of the 1930s, finding a very willing and worried audience. By 1987, however, most of the firms identified as *excellent* in this acclaimed tome were in steep decline and (with near perfect irony): "the thirty-nine companies which were reckoned *abysmal* by the six "measures of excellence" had actually outperformed the market over the same five-year period" (Wheen, 2004: 41). Nevertheless, Peters released another best-seller, *Thriving on Chaos* (1987), again with impeccable timing on "Black Monday, when the Dow Jones plummeted by 20 per cent" (ibid.: 62–3), apparently confirming his new *discovery* that the economic and business world had spun out of control, implying no company could survive without expert consultation and intervention.

Fincham and Clark argue that, since 1979, organizations have generally come to believe that they are lacking valuable, fundamental skills and qualities that are considered worthy of the cost of employing management experts to provide them (2002: 4) – confirming Parker's earlier cited suggestion that managers had descended in value from *savior* to *problem* (2002: 9). It is arguable though that during this period, management gurus, whose practices are described by certain critics as akin to "the performance of a witchdoctor" (Clark and Salaman, 1998: 49), commonly acted to identify or (re)define these deficiencies themselves (Legge, 2002: 79). They thus could be charged with having determined the problems in terms of already prepared, marketable solutions and agendas: "[those] sensitizing management to the [now] permanent flux around us ... claim to have the ability to plot a safe course" (Bloomfield and Vurdubakis, 2002: 117).

Many such publications can hence be considered as objects that extend the managerialist prerogatives of the management consulting and education industries, which themselves reflect those of the modern cultural capitalist agenda (cf. Clark and Salaman, 1998). Whether constituting "partisan writing concealed as serious advice" or being "breathlessly hysterical [and] overwhelming you with hyperbole" (Parker, 2002: 10), they tend to reinforce the dissemination of the general *neo*-liberal mantra. These three "vast libraries of propaganda" (ibid.) each then contribute to the discourse, or cultural circuits, of "new" capitalism to such a degree that there is now "no strong dividing line between business schools, consultancies and management gurus" (Thrift, 2005c: 37), and even key politicians and media sources. Thrift thus concludes that "managers are becoming better educated almost everywhere"; and as more MBA programmes are completed, they become increasingly sophisticated, leading to greater production and consumption of related "books, tapes and videos," and the packaging of these "new" capitalist objects in widely accessible "seminars" (Thrift, 1999: 44–5). This recalls the definition given earlier of discourses being *metalanguages* that can be considered "great rivers of communication" and encouragements to act, "enflamed by particular technologies" (cf. Thrift, 2005c: 24), along with the notion of actors, objects and templates coinciding to propel mass-discursive, cultural phenomena. Further, for the case of contemporary capitalism, it convincingly situates the institutions of government, and management education, consultancy and gurus as being "responsible for producing the bulk" of this process (ibid.: 37).

Complexity

The preceding arguments demonstrate the significance that management education, consultancy and gurus have impressed upon the generation and circulation of "new" capitalism. While the "new economy" could "not have taken off without this foundational cultural circuit," it is not though "the only stakeholder" (Thrift, 2005g: 116). For while what is described above deals with the major actors, objects and templates that enable the modern cultural and political circulation of capital to operate, it offers limited address to the plentiful array of other ideologically mimetic interactions at specific locales. Thrift deals with this in his discussions of "complexity theory," which he situates as a way of transcending such "problems of space" (2005d: 51). Space is especially relevant when considering capitalism, for having theorized upon *how* it circulates some attention must then be spared for *where* these processes occur. However, rather than zooming in on the capitalistic micro-practices and transactions of individuals, which are simply far too multitudinous to count, the "distribution" (ibid.) of capitalism can be better conceived of in a more abstracted, theoretical manner.

Thrift uses complexity theory to discuss the spread of capitalism, but does so by looking at the theory of complexity itself and its expansion throughout the geography community as an entity of analysis in its own right. Using it to demonstrate the operation of the theory of "circuits" which he then applies to capitalism: "I have tried to use [it] as both an object of study and as a means of making some observations about the changing sense of what is possible in Euro-American cultures" (ibid.: 59). His interest in it concerns in particular the means by which "metaphors" of complexity theory are able to "travel and gradually become a *commonplace* structure of intelligibility" (ibid.: 35, emphasis in original). Thus, by understanding how complexity has spread, one can extend these principles to the mass-discursive, cultural phenomena of "new" capital, and even happiness.

Geography is described as a discipline wary of theories that "ride roughshod over ambiguity and polarize complexities" (ibid.). Many writers on complexity theory therefore typically lay claim to a whole series of fields of study and to a "companion vocabulary which has become both technical and metaphorical: ... [including] emergent orders, self-organization, implicit order ... life at the edge of chaos, and so on" (2005d: 53). Notably, many of these notions echo the above discussions of capitalism and the Happiness Agenda as a cultural entity. Complexity theory is hence a "scientific amalgam, a rhetorical hybrid," the chief impulse of which is to understand the interactions of systems as being "greater than the sum of their parts," forming a science which favors the primacy of "processes over events, of relationships over particular entities" (ibid.: 52). This explains why when discussing space and distribution Thrift is not overly worried with detailing individual capitalist transactions. His interest in complexity theory reflects the belief that "new" capitalism is an intricate and expansive system of operation constantly evolving and self-promoting, self-organizing, and self-sustaining, comprising numerous relations that occur and spread unevenly and without uniformity. And the best way to analyse it is through reference to a myriad of sources:

> The [spread of complexity] has not ... been a simple diffusion out from a point. Rather, the propagators ... have been present in more than [one network], and these networks have therefore imported these concepts, processed them and re-exported them – sometimes even back from whence they came – showing, once again, the difficulty of controlling interpretation since the act of communication is always at one and the same time an act of dissemination.
>
> (ibid.: 53)

Although Thrift is here talking about the theory of complexity itself, as with his definition of discourse, this description above fits his view of capitalism, as the circuits by which it operates and the major driving institutional players within cannot be entirely or exclusively associated with single, specific locations. With the increasing dissemination, or translation, of capitalism throughout the globe, the burgeoning Tiger economies of the Far East and in post-Communist

Russia, for example, it is not even possible to imply it is only specific to Western, Anglo-American cultures: complexity and capitalism are international exports, imports and return-to-senders.

One prominent advocate of complexity theory, but certainly not by any means the only one, is the Santa Fe Institute, which has "attempted to produce a site which would not only do research ... but also act as a centre for ... dissemination" (Thrift, 1999: 41). Employing a "family strategy," the Institute draws from and publishes in a variety of fields including the natural sciences, archaeology, linguistics, political science, economics, history and management, attempting to make complexity theory "so well known *outside* the networks of science that it will become better respected *in* science" (ibid., emphasis added). The repetitive iteration of the main points of complexity theory throughout diverging disciplines, as established in the chapter's opening quote, acts to render them in a position of not only being ideas but becoming "unquestionable obstacles" (cf. Goodchild, 1996: 211, cited by Thrift, 1999: 31).

There are four main ways or "spaces" in which such processes occur: first, the establishment of discursive networks provide *a map of where counts*, "the main poles of innovation" such as in the case of capitalism: prominent business schools, consulting companies and influential spokespersons (ibid.: 51). Second, "the cultural valuation" of the landscapes inscribed on these maps provides *a force of identity*, whereby ideas gain credence due to the perceived value and creditability of the certain knowledge-producing organizations, or actors, such as, say, McKinsey consultants or Harvard University, from whence they emanate. Third, the spread is facilitated by *the geographies of interaction*: "In the networks of science and business, conferences symposia, seminars, workshops and other forms of face-to-face interaction are supplemented by mediated communications" (ibid.: 52). And finally, through the prominence of *a vocabulary* of "journeys, travels, maps, shifts, and transformations," an assortment of appropriations of knowledge are facilitated (ibid.: 52–3). Thrift hence uses complexity theory to legitimate his circuits argument, telling "a story of ideas" that spread throughout geography and other arenas by, as alluded to earlier, "singing a song to themselves and each other" (ibid.: 35), leading to the conclusion that the spatial dissemination of (any) mass-discursive, cultural phenomena is truly complex, in every sense of the word.

The power of subjects and objects

> He who is subjected to a field of visibility, and
> knows it, assumes responsibility for the constraints
> of power; he makes them play spontaneously upon
> himself; he inscribes in himself the power relation
> in which he simultaneously plays both roles; he
> becomes the principle of his own subjection.
>
> (Foucault, 1991: 202–3)

Two theories from the related literature that correlate with the hereto-fore explicated discussions of mass-discursive, cultural phenomena are actor-network theory (ANT) and Deleuze and Guattari's deployment of rhizomes (1988). Such a contention is supported by Thrift in the admission that his treatment of capitalism promotes an essentially "Latourian-cum-Deleuzian notion of political economy" (2001: 376). These ideas are also indicative of the work of Michel Foucault who, as in the above opening quote, considers how *objects* and *subjects* are formed in relation to and act upon one another through the mechanisms and networks of power. A discussion of these concepts is thus necessary in order to further understand how capitalism, and subsequently the Happiness Agenda, operate beyond their respective systemic, cyclical genesis and dissemination, through the process of object- and subject-ification.

Thrift openly states an interest in notions such as "actors, translation, the role of intermediaries and the agency of inscription devices" (2005d: 56), employing a lexicon often utilized by actor-network theorists. He even believes that ANT is an "ideal vehicle" as it "tells stories of continuous attempts to make networks longer," akin to capitalism's near-perpetual motion and spread throughout the globe and the notion of "unending object relations," as it travels and transmutes, engendering a "rhizomatically multiplying agenda" (Thrift, 1999: 37). As posited earlier, his conceptualization of "objects" is as a term that encompasses cultural products and social structures as well as specific technologies. Demonstrating the symbiosis between these views, one of the pioneers of ANT, Callon, puts forward a network as being the "product of interaction between a large number of diverse actors" (1991: 132), with the concept of an "actor" being used to denote both human and non-human entities (de Laet and Mol, 2000: 253), and taking the form of technological artefacts (Walsham, 2001: 47) and "companies, associations between humans, and associations between non-humans" (Callon, 1991: 140). An actor or *actant* is therefore any affective entity linked by associations to other such elements within a network: "Thus it acts: it is an actor" (ibid.).

For Thrift, the network in question is global capitalism and the actants—or actors, objects and templates – are the numerous world-wide individual, corporate and governmental players, technologies, and the politico-economic transactions, interactions and exchanges of ideas occurring between them. Considering such complex, atypical acts, adoptions and translations, capitalism, as a network, can be seen as comprising a "tentative, tendentious and uncertain" order (Thrift, 2005e: 75), wherein particular actants are "delegated" greater degrees of concentration or influence than others. For example, neo-liberal economic agendas of Western governments, ideological academic debates between Marxist, Keynesian and "New Right" scholars, pricing policies of particular companies and an individual purchasing a Sunday morning paper in a local convenience store are all potent actants operating within the network of capitalism. Yet they clearly all have differing levels of outward influence beyond their specific occurrence.

This introduces Deleuze and Guattari's (1988) concept of rhizomes. Originally this was a botanical term referring to a horizontal, usually underground stem that sends out roots and shoots from its nodes, adopted to conceptualize a genealogical explanation of the genesis of developments, ideas and movements. Rather than events occurring in complete isolation from any other or as a direct consequence of a particular trigger, this view enables the theoretical exposure and analysis of numerous, inter-related contributing causes that conspire towards specific results, each of which are connected but not all exerting an equal influence. Patton provides an explanation by contrast between *arborescent* and *rhizomatic* systems: the former is a clearly identifiable, hierarchical system in which there are "centres of significance and subjectification" with "definable boundaries and connections between all its constituent parts" (2006: 28). Examples include bureaucracies, factories, armies and schools. The latter refers to an "indeterminate" series of connections that embody the more "fluid principles" of organization found in social and cultural movements: "they have more in common with packs or bands than ... structured groups" (ibid.).

Deleuze and Guattari offer an esoteric description of rhizomes, reminiscent of Thrift's introspective discussion of complexity theory, using both themselves and their book itself as example:

> Here we have made use of everything that came within range, what was closest as well as far away ... To attribute the book subject is to overlook this working of matters, and the exteriority of their relations ... A book exists only through the outside and on the outside.
>
> (1988: 3–4)

Notably, they only afford their book credence as part of an assemblage, a network, rather than any independent function in its own right: "when one writes, the only question is which other machine [other books] the literary machine [their book] can be plugged into, must be plugged into in order to work" (ibid.). Rhizomatic systems can hence only function as a result of there being other actors, objects and templates present, resulting in the network they form being by necessity, recalling complexity theory, a totality greater than the sum of its parts. Capitalism is conceivable then as a rhizomatic network as its boundaries cannot be clearly defined. It flows to, fro and back from whence it came, adapting and changing, as a collaboration of *a*-centred actants, or "awkward and makeshift links" (Thrift, 2006: 280), that collude towards circulating their own continued holistic existence, repetition and expansion.

As indicated, such a system is of primary interest to complexity theorists. Furthermore, it is also reminiscent of a classic actor-network, wherein the term was originally intended to signify a "coordinated set of heterogeneous actors which interact ... to develop, produce, distribute and diffuse methods ... goods and services" (Callon, 1991: 133), or a series of "transformations [and] translations," within a frame of shared interests (Latour, 1999: 15). To reiterate, complexity theory is about discovering "emergent orders," and "new" capitalism is a rhizomatic network of aligned yet discrete actants that are embodiments of a socio-political and economic way or order of doing and being, that emerges out of the cumulative result of its interactions (cf. Thrift, 2005b: 2; 2005f: 94). These theories are thus complementary when considered in unison, and demonstrate from whence some of the theoretical influences behind Thrift's views of capitalism emerged. For in addition to grand historical events or cultural and economic movements, the genesis of the ideas within both his and this book can, if not must, also be considered themselves as rhizomatic and part of a network, where each entity only makes sense when considered in terms of others they have influenced and those they themselves have been influenced by.

The subject(s) of politics

Both ANT theorists (cf. Latour, 1992: 232) and Thrift (cf. 2005b: 2; 2005d: 56) describe how the actants within a rhizomatic network are unavoidably charged or *delegated* roles, functions or identities, whereby they "stand in and speak for" those who create and control them (Walsham, 2001: 47), imbibing an active political agency rather than neutrality (Cooley, 1980: 55). Further, Latour argues that non-humans particularly are designated with societal values and ethics, resulting in a networked moral code to which humans adhere (1992: 232). Bloomfield concurs, suggesting actants "are commonly instituted for the purposes of social regulation" (1995: 496), embodying and reasserting the moral and political order of the network in which they exist. Latour provides an example of human and non-human actants within a network constructing a moral code in his discussion of a car seatbelt and the integral connections between the related actants: "the red light ... the alarm ... the car ... the law ... the police" (1992: 225), all conspire to ensure drivers wear seatbelts before commencing driving. ANT thus recognizes social agents as "never located in bodies and bodies alone" (Law, 1990: 385), but co-existing in an aligned network of heterogeneous actants (Walsham, 2001: 46). Such views are clearly mirrored in the above expositions of capitalism as functioning through different actors' relations with objects and templates, whose very existence acts to reflect, maintain and reinforce the "new" ideas of how the world should be: "They do not only tell managers how to manage their organizations, they also tell them what kind of people they should become in order to be happy and morally conscious citizens with fulfilling lives" (Bos, 2000: 22, cited in Thrift, 2005f: 95–6).

Understandably, a vast number of organizational and sociological theorists have raised concerns regarding the sites and natures of the forces able to "tell" people how to *do* and *be*. Essentially, the question that must be considered is: How can it be asserted that a network of actants which comprise the cultural-economic movement labelled "new capitalism," encourage people to act in ways which are conducive to its own continuation? One of the most prominent and often referred to academics to have considered this concept is, as introduced above, Michel Foucault (Burrell, 1988: 225). While he does not refer specifically to the functional workings of capital, his discussions of power in the social realm are still appropriate to analyses of mass-discursive, cultural phenomena, especially as Thrift himself defers to his "brief writings on governmentality" when raising this issue (2005h: 133).

Foucault argued that the development of modern societies can be understood via an examination of the shifts *in* and exercise *of* power (Miller and O'Leary, 1987: 238). Expounding that in circa 1800 a form of control discernible as "disciplinary power" emerged within Western capitalist society, which penetrated "the very web of social life through a vast series of regulations and tools" (ibid.). Cooley contends that central to this period, as indeed to contemporary capitalism, was a scientistic methodology of "predictability, repeatability and quantifiability" (1980: 33). Shenhav concurs, stating that since the age of the Enlightenment Western capitalism and its agents have gone avidly "in pursuit of efficiency and reason" (1994: 277). This "peculiar" prevalent style of *rational* thought and action currently in effect (Weber, cited in Brubaker, 1984: 1) is viewed by some as a cultural process of *rationalization* (Cooper and Burrell, 1988: 93), and the organizational and societal transformation of subjects from being *"memorable"* into *"calculable"* (Martin *et al.*, 1988). Such instrumentalist and rationalist myths are often considered to be attractive to the cadres of management and politicians alike, for (as already postulated) it enables the reconstitution of society and the economy to a more efficient "arm's length" governance (recall Greer, 1994: 2), and are in collaboration with the modern Anglo-American deference to objective, scientific and easily applicable styles of thought and action.

Foucault identified four disciplinary "technologies" of control: production, power, inscriptions, and the self (Foucault, 1977, cited in Martin *et al.*, 1988: 18). These "tools" act to augment the actions of entire populations through institutional intervention via regulatory laws, and agents' internalization of promoted comportments (or templates) of behavior. Foucauldian theory argues such processes act to define, embed and reproduce asymmetrical relationships of power between certain groups (recall ANT, rhizomatic and complexity theory), forming a system that "tightly encloses all our activities," absorbing a citizen's life "completely" (Ellul, 1964: 284). Foucault's technologies can all be seen in the series of relations critical to the cultural circulation of mass-discursive, cultural phenomena, as already discussed; but it is the fourth, the "technology of the self," which is paramount to understanding how they conspire to inculcate forms of social regulation that are widely, and willingly, adopted.

To understand how a *technology of the self* functions, it is vital, as stated previously and as focused upon in Chapter 6, that the human agent is not deemed a slave to an all-dominant system of manipulation. In the section's opening quote, Foucault declares that the ultimate responsibility for the act of internalizing comportments of being lies with(in) the sentient actor, highlighting a striking correlation with Thrift: "he inscribes in himself the power relation in which he simultaneously plays both roles" (Foucault, 1991: 202–3), whereby a network of power in society, in this case capitalism, produces "both pleasures and inspirations *and* slavish compliance" (Thrift, 2005b: 2, emphasis added). For this process to work, any individual must be an active, accommodating participant: "the business organization [and society] must be made up of willing and willed subjects" (Thrift, 2005c: 34), otherwise it is rendered inert. Compliance with and internalization of the behests of a system of discipline would not function if the human agents involved were doing so merely under manifest external coercion.

It operates so influentially precisely because the manners of being requested by said system are infused with the cultural backdrop of the society in which they exist. To act as an agent of "new" capital – to work, earn, save, spend, purchase and consume – is then to be rewarded as a moral, materially rich and valued participant of modern, Anglo-American societies. Thus, what it is to count as a worthy citizen in "new" capitalist society has been "redefined" via the tools or categories of control identified by Foucault, and has become "increasingly entangled" (Thrift, 2005f: 93) with both state and personal action. Again, this explanation precludes a manipulative elite micro-managing a mindless automaton population, as the individuals "caught up" in it are necessarily complicit, aspiring and responsible contributors.

According to Thrift, much of modern capitalism is concerned with producing human subjects that are "constantly attentive" through an emphasis on the "ludic and affective" (2005b: 6), whereby "self-esteem and self-confidence" (Thrift, 2005c: 45), among other human traits such as well-being and happiness, are both sought after and catered for. The circuits of capital have then aligned themselves with a particular image of the citizen and mode of economic life, effecting a "translation between the social and cultural values of advanced liberal democracies on the one hand and the demands of industry on the other" (Rose, 1990: 108–9). This image, or behavioral template, is thus so seductive to the modern human agent as to be frequently and desirously internalized and acted out. It is of course possible for an individual to resist or refuse to comply with a dominant socio-economic movement in which they find themselves and reject the models of life on offer. But the manner in which they are packaged and instilled in the discourses of governments, organizations and individuals acts to create such an appealing way of being and doing, recompensed by both material comforts and social acceptance, that the choice to participate in this way of life is for many symptomatic of an elementary conjurer's trick: you can pick any card you like, but you will, more than likely, choose *this* one.

(Too) fast subjects

> How were you to find satisfaction in this? How were you to find peace of mind? People were aspiring to the condition of sharks, not because they were becoming more predatory but because they could not rest or they would sink and drown. The gurus of business [were] pimping for instability.
>
> (Hoffman, 2002: 57)

On its surface the rhetoric of this "new [cultural] business ecology is all nice" (Thrift, 2005g: 112). Modern capitalism provides the means for material gains, employment, fun, meaning and the improvement of virtually all aspects of human life. There is no "mechanical causality," no irrefutable obligation, but seemingly rather an economy that has gathered associations between "information technology, novelty, business revolution and youth" (ibid.). So while rebellion is possible, one might wonder why anyone would want to. The subject position afforded by and which fits most perfectly with the "new" system of capitalism is the *fast subject*. It represents a fundamental shift in commonly accepted notions of identity:

> As the number of possibilities of personhood has multiplied – through the division of labor, the sexual revolution, postcolonial imaginings, and so on – so the notions of persons as consisting of a set of complex, multivalent and more open subject positions, has taken hold.
>
> (Thrift, 1999: 56)

Resulting in contemporary Anglo-Americans now commonly aspiring to be "fractal persons" who are irreducible to a single dynamic (ibid.).

Salman Rushdie similarly asserts that the modern self is "a shaky edifice we build out of scraps, dogmas, childhood injuries, newspaper articles, chance remarks, old films, small victories, people hated, people loved" (cited in Sennett, 1999: 133). As argued earlier, in response to companies and the individuals within them having to "thrive on chaos" and survive in a state of "permanent emergency," managers have had to become "change agents' responsible for coping and leading in "a faster and more uncertain world; one in which all advantage is temporary" (Thrift, 2005g: 112) and must be constantly re-established. Previously untapped resources of knowledge are hence all "fair game" for capitalist exploitation, as the internal machinations of human subjects become "an asset class that a business must foster, warehouse, manage, constantly work upon, in order to produce a constant stream of innovation" (Thrift, 2005h: 132). The fast subject needs to be both sufficiently immutable as to withstand the "exigencies of faster and faster return" *and* flexible enough to be able to exploit any and every human capacity they possess that might enable a personal, societal or corporate competitive advantage to be forged. The executive working from a laptop on the train; the corporate provision of child day-care, dry-cleaning, masseuses and hairdressers on company sites; the utilization of seminars designed to uncover and harvest employees' creative, emotional and spiritual capabilities in the workplace: all blur work and non-work boundaries, demanding something more, something new, something different than previously required.

Thrift refers to this as:

> A new set of embodied resources being brought into the world for capitalist firms to operate on and with – resources that might well prove to be on a par with, say, the invention of ... double-entry book-keeping, filing [and] various means of production management.
>
> (Thrift, 2005h: 151).

He thus determines that this "new" embodiment of capitalism is synonymous with a fresh phase of imperialism, under which the modes of being and doing offered up to actors are a "new great map of personkind ... no doubt with *Homo siliconvalleycus* in the evolutionary lead" (ibid.). Thus, the slightly more sinister undercurrents of the contemporary, Anglo-American capitalistic way of life begin to become apparent: for, by definition, if there are to be *fast* subjects there must surely by contrast also be slower ones, as capitalism can only function if the higher echelons rest upon and exploit the surplus labor value of a large, static workforce. Furthermore, even those who are capable of embracing these behavioral and moral comportments are at risk as, alas, "this fast world cannot last" (ibid.). It, and the cultural circuits upon which it rests, promote and are largely dependent upon the hegemonic, predatory predominantly North American business model of short-term, high-profit returns (cf. Galbraith, 1996; Gray, 2002; Hutton, 2002), which is "inclined to pursue changes in work organizations and practices even though the weak might pay the price" (Sennett, 1999: 53).

There is then no guarantee that the process of producing fast subjects, which are capable of functioning in, and therefore should ideally be able to maintain, this fast "new" capitalist world, "can or will succeed" (Thrift, 2005h: 152, 136). Sennett has thus surmised: "What's peculiar about uncertainty today is that it exists without looming historical disaster; instead, it is woven into the everyday practices of a vigorous capitalism" (1999: 31). Expecting human agents to exist permanently on the brink of chaos, while ever-performing better, faster, harder and investing more and more of their human capacities into work can only ultimately result in collapse: of either many of these individuals themselves, or the cultural system that requires them. This is not an argument that economic exchange will crumble entirely, far from it, but that the managerial-ist, Anglo-American economy, like all other mass-discursive, cultural phenomena, will eventually have to adapt, as is its nature, once its present mythic and practical forms become untenable.

The cultural circuits of happiness

> Like the capitalist circuit of cultural capital, the New Age circuit depends upon a constant throughflow of new ideas, even though they are often painted as rediscoveries of older knowledge.
>
> (Thrift, 2005c: 63)

The view of capitalism outlined in the preceding intellectual pano-rama holds it as a cultural patchwork, which is phenomenological, complex, seductive, rhizomatic, non-uniform and a-centered, una-voidably bound up in how people see themselves and actively choose to participate in it. It is not all-controlling but open to appropriation, interpretation and translation, acting as a disciplinary mechanism that operates through series of micro-practices, technologies, ideas and discourses. These circulate from and throughout a network of sites, some more influential than others, providing a reflexive frame-work which, in conjunction with the numerous objects, subjects and templates that imbue its bespoke moral standing and authority, promotes the internalization of various ways of being that sustain its very existence. Being such a highly sophisticated and adaptive system, demanding only what is willingly surrendered, it is little surprise that it spreads so aptly into the very essence of modern humankind.

As discussed in the Introduction and the first section, a cardinal tenet of this book is that one of the prominent "new forms of knowl-edge" to have likewise spread on cultural circuits, manifesting, prop-agating and finding an "appropriate milieu" (recall Goodchild, 1996: 211, cited by Thrift, 1999: 31), is centered upon the human senti-ment of *happiness*. Contemporary Anglo-American interest in it can be observed, understood and analyzed in a very similar manner to capitalism – much as Thrift considers the spread of complexity – for, aside from the fact that they seem to be inextricably entwined with one another, with the very process of consumption often acting to fuel and satiate personal, corporate and political desire, they operate through congruous cultural and discursive series of relations: each is "grounded in the other, sharing a little of their glory" (ibid.).

Happiness has emerged in the modern age as a subject of philosophical, political and media debate, as justification for organizational interventions and policies, and as proof and motivation for private beliefs. It is not simply an adjective (*happy*) or a noun (*happiness*), but is very much being employed as a verb: the desire to *be happy* is arguably becoming inculcated in nigh on every facet of our cultural reality. This is occurring to such an extent that, much like being a *fast subject* of "new" capital, it "makes sense" to invest the array of financial and emotional resources at one's command towards attaining this ubiquitous societal, institutional and personal goal.

As depicted in Figure 1.1, a reimagining of Thrift's "The Expanding Institutional World of Business Knowledge" (1999: 42), the contemporary ideas and practices regarding happiness circulate throughout modernity, driven by the occurrence of three developmental, ideological *shocks*: the macro-political embracement of

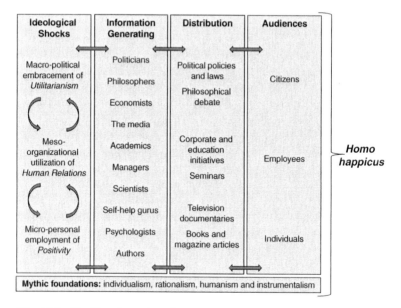

Figure 1.1   The Happiness Agenda.

LIBRARY, UNIVERSITY OF CHESTER

Utilitarianism, which informs (and is informed by) the meso-organizational utilization of Human Relations, both of which impress upon (and are impressed by) the variegated micro-personal employment of Positivity. It is in conjunction with these events, comprising an "extraordinary discursive apparatus" (recall Thrift, 2005b: 6), that the elemental *Information Generating, Distribution* and *Audiences* of the "Happiness Agenda" operate.

Following this construction and explication of the intellectual architecture with which to assess such mass-discursive, cultural phenomena, the next three chapters each will respectively focus upon one of these three identified sociological realms and the shock that has occurred within it, detailing how and why happiness has consequently come to be so pervasive and fundamental to contemporary Anglo-American society. As advocated above, they will embrace a *backward gaze*, in order to depict the current structuring of society as having emerged from a contingent and rhizomatic network of events, theories and practices, which was not inevitable but rather a consequence of particular co-ordinations of dominant *actors*, such as those in the "Information Generating" and "Audiences" columns, and *objects,* exemplified in the "Distribution" column, culminating in the promotion of affective behavioral *templates*, the subject position of *Homo happicus*. The significance of individualism, rationalism, humanism and instrumentalism throughout all these processes will also be demonstrated, to highlight the conducive, foundational theoretical and "mythic" underpinnings of Anglo-American political, organizational and psychological reality. This will ultimately provide a comprehensive, though not finite, "map of where and what counts" (cf. Thrift, 1999: 51) in the modern circulation of happiness, and account for some of the actants, vocabularies and "forces of identity" (ibid.: 52) that have propelled it to a position of such prominence.

2
A happy policy

Can political theory take this interest in happiness
seriously?

(Duncan, 2007: 86)

This chapter discusses the first chronological shock that led to the
present, peculiar structuring of the cultural circuits of happiness in
Anglo-American modernity: its nineteenth-century embracement at
a macro-political level. As contended in the previous chapter, the
societal strive toward happiness did not occur in grand sweeping
strokes, usurping the prominent hegemonies of before. Epochal,
mythic shifts in mass-discursive, cultural phenomena are rather rhizomatic, their expressive arrays of actors, objects and templates developing from a near inexhaustible catalog of causes (recall Stromberg,
1981: 12). Some of the varied yet related historical, philosophical
and political developments which seem most amenable shall thus
be proffered to provide a sustainable *history of the present* (recall
Foucault, 1991: 31), to establish both *that* happiness is embedded
in the dominant macro-political philosophy of modern Anglo-
American society and *why* this is so.

This chapter is comprised of the following sections: the first section attends to the historical transition of happiness from a philosophical to a political issue and some of the cultural conditions and
actants that facilitated such a shift, then the second section accounts
for the direct and deliberate embrace of happiness within the political realm in the guise of the theory of Utilitarianism and explicates
its core principles. The chapter then assesses the validity of the

philosophy of Utility and the manner in which it spread through geography, time and certain individuals, and relates the embodiment of utilitarian thinking in, and its appeal to, contemporary managerialist political and economic policies. Finally, the chapter then considers whether this utilitarian, neo-liberal conception of happiness is flawed in such a way as to render its utopian ideals purely theoretical, and, responding to the opening question from Duncan, ascertains why as a political project it is doggedly attempted anyway, rendering the persistent pursuit of happiness an inextricable and defining macro-political characteristic of modernity.

An ancient problem, and its modern fix

> Not that there is or ever has been that human creature breathing, however stupid or perverse, who has not on many, perhaps on most occasions of his life, deferred to [contemplating happiness].
>
> (Bentham, 1996: 13)

As indicated in the above quote, happiness is a topic of extensive human contestation. For example, Schopenhauer was rather skeptical about its "very possibility"; Kant never challenged "the pursuit" but objected to its use as a "principle for morality"; and for Nietzsche, only his "contemptible Last Men" were deemed able to "discover" it (Duncan, 2007: 86). In an attempt to demarcate some of the underlying battle lines in such an intellectual quagmire, Duncan provides two "survey-pegs" to act as opposing ends of a spectrum against which intellectual discussions can be considered. One is that of Slavoj Žižek, who hails from a "Continental tradition," and is used to demarcate the perspective that happiness is problematic, to say the least, and that attempts to manipulate it in oneself or others range from morally dubious to theoretically impossible. To contrast, the American philosopher Richard Rorty is offered, who embodies a pragmatic, instrumentalist "New World" view that aligns human progress with well-being and deems pro-active advancements in human happiness can be achieved through the machinery of politics (ibid.: 85–6).

Many contemporary affluent nations indeed espouse in their political doctrine that happiness "is and should be" attainable, and a sense of dismay or "injustice" occurs if it does not materialize (ibid.). A prominent example of this appeared on the BBC News website, where statistical evidence was reported in alarm that: "Britain is less happy [in 2005] than in the 1950s—despite the fact that we are three times richer" (Easton, 2006a). Similarly, in 2007, Reuters announced that "Americans are less happy today than 30 years ago thanks to ... a decline in ... social capital" (Babington, 2007). Such inclinations that happiness *should* be manifold (in the manner in which democratic civilizations expect their governing bodies to provide infrastructure for: holding elections, security, education, and electricity and running water for all) acts to objectify, naturalize and politicize it. This conceptualizes happiness as a supra-individual, progressive politico-ideological tool, distinct from "continental" interpretations that may by contrast seem more pessimistic. Resultantly, in modern Anglo-American society, happiness has become utilized as a teleological political campaign, the mythological history of which can now be addressed.

Pre-modern happiness

As democracy was first emerging in Athens in 450 BCE, a significant transition began to occur in mainstream early Greek philosophy, whereby the human agent became the predominant center of interest, rather than the external realm of *physis* and nature. This is known retrospectively as the *anthropocentric* period, in which: "Man [became] a problem for himself, not only as a being who thinks, but also as one who acts" (Skirbekk and Gilje, 2001: 32). During this era lived the noted and influential philosopher Socrates (c. 470–399 BCE), whose works are recorded predominantly in the writings of one of his students, Plato (c. 427–347 BCE). Socrates is considered among the pantheon of those who have: "most strongly influenced and inspired the Western spirit" (ibid.: 39). Subsequent systems of *Socratic reasoning* (or as Socrates himself referred to it as the *method of the midwife*, Jackson, 2001: 6) are approaches to inquiry in which questions are asked to expose theoretical positions to programs of logic. Socrates thereby believed and taught that objective knowledge could be attained by scrutinizing and clarifying "the concepts we have of humanity and society, such as virtue, justice, knowledge, and the good" (Skirbekk and Gilje, 2001: 47), to the extent that they can ultimately be rendered as universal and unchangeable. It was hence only by learning the dialogically refined and rationalized knowledge pertaining to human virtue and goodness that individuals could ever be happy: "'Now isn't it clear', I asked, 'that the wickedest man will also prove to be the unhappiest?'" (Socrates, cited in Plato, 1994: 336).

Plato shared his teacher's beliefs in the existence of rational and objective logics conceivable to the human mind, however, he placed less faith in the average layperson's ability to master the complexities of those relating to the paragon of virtue. Consequently, due to the inherent difficulty of such ideas and the relative lack of the required intellectual ability, discipline and training among the contemporaneous general populace, most would be unable to achieve adequate insight into the ideas and therefore "not ... be able to be virtuous and live a good and happy life" by independent means (Skirbekk and Gilje, 2001: 56). It was upon such a rationale that Plato's elitist belief in the governance over the ill-educated many by the enlightened few was founded: "the philosopher king lives seven hundred and twenty-nine times more pleasantly than the tyrant, and the tyrant the same amount more painfully than the philosopher king" (Plato, 1994: 352). Plato was hence quite *anti*-democratic by modern standards, and shared with Socrates a belief that personal happiness was a benefit earned by those who sought and mastered the difficult knowledge and act of being virtuous. Among those whom he influenced, it was thus not considered as a particular end in itself that should and even could be directly striven for.

Subsequent to Socrates' execution by the Grecian rulers, an event which impacted his disciple greatly, Plato spoke widely on his belief that:

> In a healthy city-state power should be placed in the hands of those who are competent—not in the hands of the people and not in the hands of an ... iniquitous absolute ruler. This could be accomplished by having a universal education system in which everyone [is assigned roles] according to their abilities.
>
> (Skirbekk and Gilje, 2001: 56)

He thus advocated the establishment and maintenance of three hierarchical social classes (supported by a sub-class of slave labor) composed of: rulers; administrators and the military; and those tasked with producing the material requirements of society. As "we have different natural aptitudes, which fit us for different jobs" (ibid.: 59), Plato felt this division would benefit all by the mutual and complementary interaction of the three classes. Furthermore, he desired the abolition of the social institutions of private property and family life for the two higher classes, those with political power, as they represented the promotion of self-interest to the detriment of the common good: "Family life 'privatizes' its members. Riches are the origin of envy and conflict. Both weaken the sense of community in society" (ibid.: 58). It was then the communal with which Plato was primarily concerned, as he made no allowance for what an individual may wish for themselves over what society demands of them:

> Those who complain that there is too little freedom in the ideal state have misunderstood what is their own good; namely, that freedom is freedom to realize one's own life, and that one can only realize one's life in society.
>
> (ibid.: 59)

This concurs with Plato's above rejection of the notion that an individual not learned in philosophical rigor might facilitate their own happiness. While it is not the explicit concern or mythic foundation of such a (theoretical) society's leaders to provide universal happiness, it is, however, considered to result symptomatically as a by-product of the deliberate and careful orchestration of a harmonious population. As, for Plato, human happiness is not a sum derived from an aggregation of the individual citizens' sense of well-being within society, but a state provided to them by it.

Aristotle (c. 384–322 BCE), a student at Plato's Academy, also considered the philosophy of happiness and shared the view that human beings are only able to live a worthy life within the community (ibid.: 67), but was convinced to a palpably less degree than his mentor. While Plato was an *idealist*, believing resolutely that: "There's no existing form of society good enough for the philosophic nature, with the result that it gets warped and altered, like a foreign seed sown in alien soil" (Plato, 1994: 233), Aristotle was far more of a *realist*. He endeavored to investigate and improve existing forms of social and political organization, rather than decry their failings against an abstracted and idealized image of perfection. He hence developed key ontological differences, believing that virtue, goodness and happiness are not entirely independent of humankind, as in the Platonic realm of *The Forms*, but rather socially produced "*in* the way human beings live" (Skirbekk and Gilje, 2001: 80, emphasis in original). For Aristotle, in divergence from Plato and Socrates, the path to happiness was not one exclusively trodden by those schooled in appropriate philosophical reasoning, but was open to any who were able to fulfil their purpose in society (ibid.). In place of the belief, or myth, of there being a single, universal and knowable absolute regarding human happiness, he favored the conception that the good life does not have to follow the exact same format for everyone. He did, however, consider it to be beyond the grasp of those suffering prolonged physical discomfort, parting company once again with Plato, who felt that: "both pleasure and pain are irrelevant to happiness" (ibid.: 81).

A relative contemporary of Aristotle who somewhat agreed with him on this point was Epicurus (c. 341–271 BCE), who preached in the Athenian agora that "the sole source of happiness is pleasure" and that every action we take should be conducted for the purpose of its elicitation (Schoch, 2006: ii). He also believed resolutely that the good life is one of "well-being and an absence of pain and suffering" (Skirbekk and Gilje, 2001: 91). Despite subsequent (misguided) condemnation from philosopher rivals of inciting moral depravity, Epicurean philosophy is actually an advocacy of discipline, restraint and the renouncement of luxury and sensual indulgence, as pleasure, and therefore happiness, come from the absence of desire rather than attempts to satiate it. Epicurus believed that to maximize well-being and minimize suffering, the comparative values and effects of each must be *calculated*, a "province" described by Skirbekk and Gilje as that of "the cultivated self-conscious hedonist!" (ibid.). Epicureans were not then "sensualists" concerned merely with justifying self-gratification and over-indulgence, but rather were overly cautious and deliberate in their acts, believing it is only pleasure that we are personally in control of that can guarantee happiness. To this end, and diverging markedly from the social perspectives of Socrates, Aristotle and Plato, Epicureanism deprecated all political and even religious activity due to its ability to cause worry and emphases on that which is external to individual interests: "[All that] keeps people from breaking the law is a fear of punishment; that is, fear of pain. Everything is based on individual pleasure" (ibid.: 92).

While recoiling from such individualistic philosophizing, both Plato and Aristotle conceded that their conceptions of the validity and political health of the ideal state presupposed a relatively small society. But with the gradual appropriation of many of the Greek city-states into the expanding Hellenistic-Roman Empire, spanning temporally from circa 300 BCE to CE 400, most eventually became swollen geographically and demographically, assuming culturally, religiously and linguistically diverse populations. Such developmental environmental conditions ultimately facilitated, or even necessitated, significant changes in popular mythic conceptions of the power and nature of citizenry and templates of human agency. As the enactment of authority came to be concentrated in centralized locales, "the people" consequently experienced "increasing political powerlessness" in their lives (ibid.: 89). This manifested under early Hellenism at an intellectual level in "A general tendency to refrain from philosophical speculation about society ... and to concentrate on one thing: how can a person secure his or her own happiness?"(ibid.: 90).

Speculations on happiness remained then generally philosophic, but became increasingly individualized, as seen with Epicureanism, as the constitution of the political states in which a majority of Western people lived altered quite dramatically. Skirbekk and Gilje go to the extent of suggesting that: "there was a universal change from concern with man-in-community to concern with the isolated, private individual" (ibid.).

Following such a mandate, Seneca (c. 4 BCE–65 CE), a Spanish-born citizen of the Roman Empire—who was unjustly banished to Corsica by the Emperor Claudius only to be returned, made complicit in murder and ultimately ordered to commit suicide by the succeeding Emperor Nero—composed dialogues advocating a Stoic detachment and indifference in the face of the inescapably unjust nature of life. He found supposing one's state of mind as being entirely independent from environment, would bring "happiness even in circumstances more dreadful than [one] could have imagined" (Schoch, 2006: iv). He thus believed, similarly to Socrates and Plato, that the requisite condition for happiness is the commencement of a virtuous life, but conversely saw this as being entirely and irrefutably distinct from all external circumstances (Skirbekk and Gilje, 2001: 93). This resonated with much of the general population in the Hellenistic-Roman period, as their ability to control external phenomena such as illness or crop failure was relatively impotent. Analytically, a clear divide with the preceding Greek ideological ethos of ethics being married with social and political concerns is quite evident then as, under Senecan philosophy: "Each person was to cultivate the self, independently of society and environment" promoting the ideas of a "private morality, divorced from society" (ibid.: 93).

Medieval happiness

In addition to this developing focus on the individual, the generalized apathy and resignation from philosophizing upon the constitution of society engendered social conditions across Western Europe in which emergent popular *religious* desires also came to arise. One school of thought that sought to bridge the gap between philosophy and the spiritual longing of many people was Neo-platonism, the goal of which was to liberate the spirit from its mortal frame of the body so that: "the personal soul can experience the all-encompassing union with the world-soul" (Skirbekk and Gilje, 2001: 98). Based on third century CE interpretations of the teachings of Plato, it pronounced that humanity existed separately to an eternal and supreme transcendent realm of being, from whence it came and toward which freed souls could return upon corporeal death. A number of the key concepts of this movement, such as an other-worldly realm of existence, the absence of good being the source of evil and that this situation originates from human sin, however, were subsequently reiterated with greater gravitas and effect in ensuing more formalized, widespread and politically motivated mythologies: "only with Christianity (in the West anyway), with its message of a living, personal God and a redeeming paradise, did the religious longing find a satisfying answer for a larger group of people" (ibid.).

By the fourth century, Christian dogma had achieved a relative stranglehold over the "rivers of dialogue and discourse" (recall Thrift, 2005c: 24) flowing around Western Europe, emanating from the Vatican City in Rome, being officially consecrated as the official religion of the Roman Empire. A major facet of its spread and acceptance, in addition to being deliberately propelled by the cultural and political might of Roman hegemony, was its systematic and near-universal appeal: "it proclaimed hope for everyone" (Skirbekk and Gilje, 2001: 109). In spite of human difference, frailty, suffering and political powerlessness, all could find salvation through embracing specific preachings and requirements. This was particularly efficacious as life for the majority in this period was far from homogeneous or secure. Social governance had evolved into a collection of feudal states, in which the head of a particular principality (be it a king or emperor) and the nobility therein negotiated a contract of mutual benefit. Fiefdoms were established, granting the vassal nobles authority and power in exchange for allegiance, military support and taxes. Further, a contract was also effected between the vassals and the peasants who lodged on their bestowed lands, whereby "the vassal was to protect the people of his fief, and the people, in return, were to give a portion of their harvest to the vassal" (ibid.: 111). Existence for the majority was thus full of hardship and eked from the land, and the mythic framework of Christianity's post-mortem reward offered a way by which to navigate and justify such conditions, that may otherwise have seemed impracticable.

Notably, this religious movement was essentially *catholic* in nature: grounded in faith and tradition, and outwardly accepting of a philosophic approach to life as it was deemed to have been created by God. It was taught that advocates of Christianity should therefore engage with an investigated approach to the nature of existence, demarcating a synthesis with the aforementioned Neo-platonism, forged in particular by Saint Augustine. It promoted the official recognition of: history as a linear development, the universe having been created by God from nothing, and mankind as residing in the center (ibid.: 114). Remaining dominant between approximately CE 300 and 1200, this amalgamated, discursive network of actants, dubbed Catholicism, reigned supreme in Europe for most of what has retrospectively come to be known as the Middle Ages.

Similar to the appropriative acts of Neo-platonism, Aristotle was also effectively rediscovered in the thirteenth century by Western Christians through the theological works of St Thomas Aquinas (1225–1274), and actively ingratiated with the dominant philosophies of the Roman Catholic Church (ibid.: 110). Like Aristotle, Aquinas considered humankind to be essentially social creatures, and that living in society is a condition of one's ability to *actualize*: "a natural activity that allows the realization of human attributes" (ibid.: 125). This represented a series of rekindled commonalities between early Greek and Christian thought, with Aquinas proclaiming:

It is true that human beings can lead a virtuous and happy life without revelation. And it is the statesman's task to prepare the way for this realization, whether that statesman (the prince) is a

Christian or not. But beyond virtue and happiness stands the final goal: salvation.

(ibid.: 125)

Late Middle Ages society was therefore typically governed by two sources of authority, each demanding loyalty: the State and the Church. Significantly, the agency of the individual was still superseded by the legitimacy of both the social and the religious. One's most pressing duty was then commonly conceived of as being in service to these, sometimes cognizant, sometimes conflicting, parties, and not to oneself. While universal human happiness was increasingly being recognized as possible and even desirable, it was still not widely embraced as the ultimate, actionable goal of society.

In the sixteenth century, however, the mythic structure underpinning the Roman Catholic Church suffered a severe and lasting ideological assault. The desire of the contemporaneous English monarch Henry Tudor VIII (1491–1547) to divorce his first wife, the devoutly Catholic Catherine of Aragon (1485–1536), for "The Whore" Anne Boleyn (c.1501–1536) coincided with the actions of Martin Luther (1483–1546), a German monk and avidly motivated church reformer, renowned for nailing his new Thesis to the door of the Castle Church in Wittenberg. Both sought to break free of the far-reaching supremacy of the Papacy and, through their respective acts and influences, contributed to the Christian faith becoming officially split between Catholicism and Protestantism, resulting in a divisive revolution "that turned the Church's view of tradition and of faith and salvation upside down" (Skirbekk and Gilje, 2001: 139–40). Such an act was a clear *reformation* of the dominant ideas regarding the Bible and individuals' faith, enacted against Catholic tradition and the Pope. Under the resulting breakaway Lutheran or Church of England faith, the individual stood in greater isolation than ever before in relation to God and society, no longer needing the mediatory covenant of the Church. Personal faith alone was felt sufficient medium by which to interact with the highest realm of being.

An Enlightened ideal

According to Max Weber, the Reformation contributed markedly to further dramatic sociological shifts across the seventeenth century in the traditional, socially accepted conceptions of society, duty and agency, and "prepared the way for an ethic which legitimized a new rational way of life" (Skirbekk and Gilje, 2001: 406). Under subjects' increasingly individualized relations with God, one another and themselves, engagement in work came to be deemed as essentially vocational and most purposive in the quest for social harmony, religious salvation and personal happiness: "In this way, Protestantism created what Weber called a 'worldly asceticism' [that] restructured personality" (ibid.).

Weber was though quite critical of such processes, warning that heightening rationalization was leading to a general *anomic* "loss of meaning" (cf. Durkheim, 1984). In the absence of a communal and unifying set of ethics, "it was the struggle of everyone against everyone else" (Skirbekk and Gilje, 2001: 407). These developmental conditions, however, afforded opportunity for these new mythologies to rise, as the increasingly avowed rationalistic and atomistic, or individualist, perspectives abounded throughout Western society.

Such transitions arguably represented a relatively distinct and decisive break with many of the prominent anxieties and interests which had reigned previously. Since the Socratic age, European thought had periodically fluctuated between individualist and humanist episteme in relation to considerations of the good and happy society. But with the subsequent advancement of the *Age of Enlightenment*, such ruminations were effectively transferred with great effect from the contemplative philosophic to the actively political realm. Evans states that the thinkers of the Enlightenment were "fascinated with the emotions," believing their care and consideration to be vital to individual and social existence (2002: xi). This period, stemming from the mid-eighteenth and throughout the nineteenth centuries, is also referred to as the *Age of Reason*, and is intimately connected with widely burgeoning attention toward social change and scientific progress, democracy, rationality, human rights, the rejection of absolutism and monarchist power, and gross political upheaval, resulting, in one extreme expression, with the French Revolution in 1789 (Skirbekk and Gilje, 2001: 242).

Some historians go so far as to suggest that to speak in this context solely of a *French* revolution, typified by the image of the bourgeois aristocracy being condemned to the guillotine, is, however, too reductive. As what was occurring on the world stage was more a Western or Atlantic ideological revolution, affecting the

English colonies in America (who also revolted in the American War of Independence between 1775 and 1783), extending "through revolutions in Switzerland, the Low Countries, and Ireland," and from France (who had imported English ideas of liberalism and individual rights) through to Holland, Germany and Italy: "the [French] Revolution produced ideas for which the whole Western world was ready" (Stromberg, 1981: 14).

Academic journals promoting rationalism avidly collated works on all known aspects of knowledge and universities were modernized, as both humanistic and scientistic disciplines began to develop markedly, resulting in an historical period in which "a new intellectual era had emerged" (Skirbekk and Gilje, 2001: 243). These new principles of an instrumentally rationalized humanism soon increased in popularity and influence as the twentieth century began to loom. Throughout Europe, power was beginning to transfer from the landed oligarchy to the middle and industrious classes, and social values, political ideas and business practice all increasingly began to show signs of embracing the enhancing "scientization of society" (Stromberg, 1981: 55).

There were of course various counter-movements and opposing forces, such as Edmund Burke's accusation that the Enlightenment "invited the Godless to slaughter each other" (ibid.: 13), but these programs carried on with widespread appeal:

> And the ideological conflict was the notion of human rights and liberalism (Locke) in opposition to the absolute monarchy and the traditional privileges of the nobility. Moreover, natural science (Newton) was opposed to religion and the power of the priests. The philosophers of the Enlightenment opposed reason to tradition, and, by means of reason, hoped to achieve happiness and progress in the struggle against privileges and ignorance.
>
> (Skirbekk and Gilje, 2001: 243)

The period denoted as the Enlightenment thereby encompassed clear and dramatic shifts in the constitution and interests of society, with Stromberg referring to the period of 1800–1850 as "the most revolutionary half-century in history up to that time" (1981: 64). Herzberg similarly affords that the Industrial Revolution, which he locates in the same era, resulted in industry becoming the principal dominant powerhouse in society from this point, rather than preceding religious or Renaissance ideals: "The manager [was] the dominant figure of the contemporary scene" (cited in Townley, 2002: 549–50). Bakan concurs, stating: "The corporation ... essentially replaced the church in terms of who you are ... [it wants] obedient constituents that ... pay their dues and follow the rules" (2004: 134).

A new sense of psychological unity, a novel, attractive manner in which simply to *be* in the (particularly Anglo-American) world, thus came to be promulgated, through which individual harmony with the newly industrializing, democratizing and scientized politico-economic environment could be found. The associated cultural myth structure and subject positions promoted the view that the human being has "positive potentialities" that can be harnessed toward economic interests in the "spirit of the entrepreneur" (ibid.). Human nature had therefore become re-defined at a generalized level, once again, by the culmination of certain actants in positions of relative political and social influence, through the substantiation of numerous actors, objects and templates, with principles of reason increasingly replacing those based on faith, and actions being considered "right" if they produced the most good consequences rather than because an "authoritative source had commanded it" (Tipton, 1984: 282–3, cited in Heelas, 2002: 79). The entwined, epiphenomenal macro-social dialogues of industrialization and the Enlightenment calling for a new discourse through which humanity could be conceived hence offered an ideal opportunity for certain contemporaneous champions, in the guise of *Utilitarian* philosophers and social reformers, to emerge center-stage.

The utility of happiness

> The offspring of that strange genius ...
>
> (Stromberg, 1981: 66)

Jeremy Bentham (1748–1832) was a British jurist and critic of society who campaigned passionately for legal reforms, and is widely considered the father of Utilitarianism. Bizarrely, at his own request, his preserved body, topped with a wax head, is on display in a wooden cabinet at University College, London. For the centenary and 150th anniversaries of the college he was reportedly brought to the meeting of the College Council, where he was listed as "present but not voting" (Layard, 2005: 4; cf. Stromberg, 1981: 70).

Bentham belonged to both rationalist and humanist traditions, rejecting the notions of natural rights, believing rather that the sole justification and purpose for those in authority to enact political change stem from human needs in relation to pain and pleasure (Skirbekk and Gilje, 2001: 263): "it is for them alone to point out what we ought to do" (Bentham, 1996: 11). He believed utmost in liberalism, individualism, rational action and *utility*, by which he meant: "that property in any object, whereby it tends to produce benefit, advantage, pleasure, good or happiness," or to prevent the contrary occurring, for the benefit of "the party whose interest is considered" (ibid.: 12).

Since its inception, Bentham's work has understandably been often associated with the notion of *hedonism*, as at the core of the "hedonic thesis" is the principle that *pleasure is intrinsically good* (Feldman, 1997: 9). In moral philosophy, the term then denotes the position that the "good life" *should* be one which is pleasurable, and in psychology it stands for the theory that the act of instrumentally seeking pleasure is the main motivator of human behavior (Veenhoven, 2003a: 437). Overskeid similarly defines "psychological hedonism" as "[a] very old assumption [that] all action aims at attaining pleasure for the agent," and correlates it as far back as the works of Aristippus of Cyrene and, as discussed above, Epicurus (2002: 77). He further suggests that the "classic Greek philosophers" and subsequent British thinkers of Bentham's era each assumed close connections between their hedonic beliefs regarding causation and ethicality. Hedonists are therefore: "positive about pleasure and ... pluck [its] fruits ... when possible" (ibid.), rendering it a morally acceptable comportment of behavior under utilitarian mythology.

There is, however, much debate regarding the merits of such a perspective; some praise the purposeful pursuit of pleasure as a natural and healthy endeavor while others equate it with overindulgence and moral decay (recall the spurious criticisms of the Epicureans). In popular culture, hedonism has been used to convey both connotations of "good taste and the art of living well" as well as "addiction, superficiality, irresponsibility and egoism" (ibid.). This is because it regards basic "desires and emotions" as the driving "principal proximal causes" of human action in search for a self-orientated happiness (ibid.: 90). However, while research into hedonistic attitudes at the individual level often correlate with, for example, frequent sexual gratification and the use of stimulants, their relationship reportedly follows an inverted U-curve: "spoilsports and guzzlers are less happy than modest consumers" (Veenhoven, 2003a: 437).

A strong advocate of such a perspective, Bentham is described as belonging "to the later Enlightenment and never [having] departed from it in essential spirit" (Stromberg, 1981: 66; cf. Layard, 2005: 5). His intellectual lineage draws from earlier figures, such as Locke, Hume, Smith, and the French thinker Helvétius, from whom he learnt: "that good government is that which secures the greatest happiness of the people" (Stromberg, 1981: 67; cf. Skirbekk and Gilje, 2001: 263). Where Bentham stood apart from his predecessors, however, is the manner in which he, similarly to psychological hedonism, systematically and proactively attempted to develop an overarching system for calculating and promoting what provides the most pleasure, towards a philosophical system with "profound practical implications" (Rosen, 1996: xxxii). Along with his cohorts, he proposed radical changes in British society, including the abolition of the aristocracy and monarchy, the reduction of the two Houses of Parliament into one, a complete overhaul of penury and schooling systems, and ardent petitioning for democratic and universal suffrage:

> In behalf of these proposals, the followers of Bentham, including James Mill and many others, wrote pamphlets, edited magazines tried to elect members of Parliament, and in general crusaded eagerly, inspired by their belief that they had at last found the exact science of government.
>
> (Stromberg, 1981: 67)

Utilitarians of Bentham's era hence asserted that "concrete liberties must be embodied in legislation to be meaningful" (ibid.: 68), and wished to enact such change in the government ministries of healthcare, finance, trade, policing and indigence relief (Rosen, 1996: xxxix). Bentham could then be described as the nineteenth-century epitome of Rorty's *New World* progressivist, pragmatic and practical approach to happiness. Never able to accept "confused thinking" (ibid.: xlvi) and wishing to "get rid of metaphysical rubbish" in politics, law and social theory (Stromberg, 1981: 68), Bentham concentrated on enacting tangible, measureable and scientifically founded changes for improvement towards an exact "moral science" (Bentham, 1996: 11). He demonstrated how "the greatest happiness for the greatest possible number [lends] itself to individualist rational-choice theories" (Duncan, 2007: 89). One's individual happiness, how it can be measured, and securing the collective maximization of it, hence began to emerge as contemporaneously prominent, political concerns in British industrialized, Enlightened and Utilitarian society—three frameworks many regarded as "but different aspects of a single revolution" (Stromberg, 1981: 1).

A calculus of felicity

Echoing Epicurean philosophy, Bentham believed with certainty that human happiness was amenable to precise measurement, the expression of which depended on four key circumstances: (1) the intensity of the pleasure or pain; (2) how long it lasts; (3) how certain it is that either will occur; and (4) how experiences interfere with one another (cf. Skirbekk and Gilje, 2001: 263; Bentham, 1996: 38). He deemed that these factors enabled the calculation of either pleasure or pain—a calculus of felicity—when considered in and of themselves, but when a value is required in terms of its relationship with any *act* by which it is produced then the *fecundity* ("the chance of it being followed by a sensation of the same kind") and the *purity* ("the chance it has of *not* being followed by sensations of the *opposite* kind") must also be included (Bentham, 1996: 38–9, emphasis in original). These were considered to be exclusively the properties of events that led to pleasure or pain and not of the specific sensations themselves. Further, should the required valuation extend beyond the level of the individual to that of a group, a seventh circumstance must be accounted for, the *extent*: "that is the number of persons who are affected" (ibid.).

According to Bentham, in order to garner a precise understanding of how the interests of an individual or a community are affected by a particular act, the researcher must "begin with any one person of those whose interests seem to be most affected by it" and record the "value" of each "distinguishable" pleasure and pain that appear "in the first instance"; followed by those which occur subsequently, and tally them in a cost/benefit table: "The balance, if it be on the side of pleasure, will give the good tendency of the act upon the whole ... if on the side of pain, the bad tendency of it upon the whole" (ibid.: 39–40).

This method is then to be repeated in a cumulative process, with measurement taken from each member of the community in question. Mercifully, Bentham recognized that such an investigation could not actually be logistically carried out for absolutely all members of any given population or in regards to every moral, legislative and judicial judgement. But he did believe firmly that as a system of investigation it was methodologically and empirically robust: "In all this there is nothing but what the practice of humankind, wheresoever they have a clear view of their own interest, is perfectly conformable to do" (ibid.).

In terms of defining what actually constitutes a pleasure and a pain, a necessary process if each is to be identified in the human subjects of his investigations, Bentham goes to great lengths to categorize both those which are *simple*, and cannot be resolved into more, and those which are *complex*, which are further reducible into other expressions. Pleasure consists of an appreciation of: sense, wealth, skill, amity, a good name, power, piety, benevolence, malevolence, memory, imagination, expectation, association, and relief. Contrastingly, and yet with many repetitions, pains comprise awareness of: privation, the senses, awkwardness, enmity, an ill name, piety, benevolence, malevolence, memory, imagination, expectation and association (ibid.: 42). Many of these are also further sub-categorized into their component parts and granted independent definitions and examples. They can also be defined as either *extra-* or *self-regarding*, depending on whether, by default or in a unique circumstance, they necessarily entail reference to a simple or complex pleasure or pain in another human being.

To complicate matters further, causality of the pain or pleasure experienced does not abide exclusively within the agent, as they are rather described as responses to external factors that are mediated by their specific "degree or quantum of sensibility" (ibid.: 51). This renders supra-psychological influences as a constant that are only varied in their effect by an individual's specific disposition: "this proportion will in different minds be different" (ibid.). The principal circumstances referred to are: health, bodily imperfections, strength, hardiness, quality and quantity of knowledge, firmness and steadiness of mind, moral and religious sensibility and biases, and sanity. Others relegated to "secondary" include: rank, education, climate, lineage, the government of the time, and any religious fraternity.

Such factors, "all or many of them," must be considered "upon any occasion any account is taken of any quantity of pain or pleasure, as resulting from any cause," in order to judge the relative degree being experienced by an individual (ibid.: 69). This calculation can then, apparently, be used to enact rewards, punishment or social legislation depending on the calculated impact, whether positive or negative, upon a person, community or entire population, equal to the cumulative *quantum* of their reaction. Social well-being is therefore a matter of measurement and compilation, in direct opposition to the beliefs of Plato; and Utilitarianism is then, in a sense, a statistical and political method by which to consider the collective at the level of the individual.

The utility of Utility

> His method of attacking social reform piecemeal, assailing it with factual research, and avoiding large nebulous slogans ... seemed to suit the English genius—individualistic, empirical, mistrustful of general ideas and metaphysics.
>
> (Stromberg, 1981: 69)

Bentham's rational and instrumental attempt to create an "objective measuring-stick" (Stromberg, 1981: 68) that considered social welfare as the sum total of calculable units of individual happiness, is very reminiscent of a calculation of profit (Skirbekk and Gilje, 2001: 263). Yet, while balance sheets typically deal with uniform and directly comparable units, his mathematical representation, addition and subtraction of feelings offers little to no sufficient solution as to how discrete subjective valuations can be reconciled with one another objectively (ibid.: 264). In his original works, Bentham compounds this confusion by using phrases such as *estimating* and *general tendency* when referring to producing an *exact account* (1996). This is, however, fraught with obvious problems: "How can we compare the value of pleasure in the quiet enjoyment of good food and the wild ecstasy after passing an examination?" (Skirbekk and Gilje, 2001: 264). Duncan similarly asserts that viewing happiness as the "absence of misery and presence of good feelings" is somewhat reductive and overly two-dimensional, and accounts poorly for harmful pleasures such as drug taking (2007: 96).

Additional problems also arise in Bentham's distinctions between the individual and the collective. Pleasure, often considered in the context of Utilitarianism as happiness, is specific to individual human agents: "The state or the community can have neither pleasure nor pain" (Skirbekk and Gilje, 2001: 264). However, the concept of utility relates to "desirable consequences," wherein the criteria for what are *good* or *desirable* actions reflect those that will benefit the greatest number of a given population, even if at the expense of an individual. It is here that the theory of utility can be seen as potentially in conflict with notions of universal suffrage and justice, as it could, speaking theoretically, then be used to justify the persecution of a minority for the benefit of the remaining majority. Any justificatory generalization akin to *the greatest good for the greatest number* necessarily entails the exclusion of those that do not fit in with the myths or discourse of the prevailing social norms: "Punishment of one or of a few individuals, which in itself inflicts pain, is … just if the result, as a whole, provides greater pleasure" (ibid.: 265; cf. Duncan, 2007: 96). Even Bentham's leading disciple, James Mill (1773–1836), who argued for poverty laws, universal education and an elected, fully democratic governing assembly based on general voting rights, had contrastingly limited sympathy for the rights of the minority, who, for him, were: "the over-privileged nobility and the priesthood" (Skirbekk and Gilje, 2001: 265).

Further, Bentham's emphasis on the sovereignty of the individual was so extreme that he eventually rejected all conceptual terms such as *rights*, *general prosperity* and *property*, as he felt they concealed the true nature of social reality. Which he believed was reducible to: "man is at all times and in all places seeking the same goals (pleasure) and driven by the same forces (seeking pleasure)" (ibid.). This de-emphasizes the impacts of networks of power, discourse and social construction, and renders humanity as entirely *a*social and *a*historical beings:

> History, for Bentham, is a collection of traditions, habits, and customs that can justify their existence only if they can withstand a critical investigation based on the principle of the greatest possible happiness for the greatest possible number of particular individuals.
>
> (ibid.)

Detractors hence considered Bentham's methodology for a calculus of felicity as "a failure and an illusion" (Stromberg, 1981: 68). Despite this though, the banner and cause of Utilitarianism spread on the coat-tails of Enlightenment and industrial thinking far beyond its native English shores, throughout Europe and as far as Russia and South America (ibid.: 69), with governance that advocated individualism, economic liberalism and rational action as a way to inculcate "collective harmony," as "when all seek to maximize their pleasure, it is for the best for all individuals" (Skirbekk and Gilje, 2001: 265), becoming a near-globally debated political issue.

Many French thinkers, for example, rejected some of the individualistic foundations in favor of stressing a more directly social principle, viewing "society" not merely as a generic label for the sum of its component parts. But Bentham's mythic "creed of self-interest" and belief in the right to private property struck a special accord with the budding English bourgeoisie of the industrializing nineteenth century, who were emerging as a wealthy middle class, able to own and command their own capital (to borrow a Marxian description), from between the poorer working classes and underclasses and the landed gentry: "Certainly there were builders of wealth in this vigorous morning of the Industrial Revolution, very proud of their achievements, inclined to be scornful of those who contributed less" (Stromberg, 1981: 55). Benthamite principles which could be used to support the individual accumulation of affluence thus gained great credence among this newly establishing power base, with London's influential publication *The Economist* dogmatically preaching that "the sum of private interests is always the same as the public interest" (ibid.: 102). The mid-Victorian era in Britain hence came to be virtually synonymous with: "Middle-class domination, comfortable bourgeois virtues, industrialism and free trade, political stability with an undercurrent of working class distress" (ibid.: 101).

Despite her foreign and domestic critics, Britain advocated and exported the notions of a liberalist, *laissez-faire* government approach to free markets and trade, little to no taxes, no labor unions or legal protection for adult male workers, the promotion of individual private enterprise and, further pre-empting the contemporary age, the prerogative of self-help (ibid.). Fueled in part by booming industry and wealth, the spread and influence of the British Empire (both inherited and expanded by Queen Victoria) stretched from the tips of Greenland and Canada down the mainland of North and South America, to the Falklands, the Caribbean, across the Mediterranean, Southern Africa, India, Australia and Hong Kong. Even with the 13 colonies of the Americas declaring independence back in 1776, as late as the 1920s, the British still held influence over approximately one-quarter of the world's population and land mass. Unsurprisingly this history of British rule throughout the world—spawning the phrase "the sun never sets on the British Empire"—left a significant legacy in legal, educational, economic and governmental practices; languages, sports and military bases; and, compellingly, socio-political utilitarian ideologies and mythic conceptions of happiness.

An "ancestor of English Socialism" (Stromberg, 1981: 107)

The strain of utilitarianism that helped drive the political, industrial and social change experienced during the first half of the nineteenth century was, however, far from eternal. The changes experienced primarily aided the middle and newly wealthy classes, arguably to the relative deprivation of those lower down the social hierarchy. While poverty laws and voter enfranchisement may have been improved to a degree, those benefiting most were certainly the ones willing and able to embrace the hedonistic individualist and instrumentalist myths that securing their own wealth, well-being and happiness was key to pulling up that of the nation.

John Stuart Mill (1806–1873), son of James Mill, personifies in microcosm the shifting political and social concerns of this ideologically turbulent time: "Bentham's creed of self interest [had] doubtless gone out of style in the twentieth century" (Stromberg, 1981: 69). Described as "the most celebrated and symbolic" thinker of mid-Victorian England (ibid.: 106), Mill Junior was raised according to the principles of his father in a strict Benthamite tradition (ibid.; cf. Skirbekk and Gilje, 2001: 266). But affected by the tangible rising outrage over living and working conditions for the lower classes, he rebelled. While retaining the scientistic and anti-metaphysical mindset of his predecessors, he strove against British *individualist liberalism*, being influenced by French philosophy, towards a more *social* variation. He embodied a growing societal trend wishing to attend to the increasing deprivation of the working classes, fueled perhaps by a fear of political unrest in the form of Marxist revolt and, also, from a sincere humane compassion (ibid.: 266).

The lower classes had little to no formal representation in Parliament, with the Conservatives traditionally being concentrated around the land-owning nobility and the Liberals concerned with industrialists and businessmen (cf. the formation of the Labour Party in 1908 by trade unions). However, in 1867, the Conservative Government granted many workers the right to vote, as liberals joined the swelling tide of more socialistic thinking, hoping to gain the "broad support of the people" (ibid.), a move retrospectively given the moniker "the leap in the dark" (Saville, 1987: 8). As consequence, the theories of Bentham *et al.* regarding the relationship between the individual and the state "had to be rewritten", with the political focus on rampant individualism eventually becoming modified towards more inclusive and humanistic thought (ibid.).

A *neo*-utilitarianism hence began to emerge, with John Stuart Mill especially being quite critical of Bentham's quantitative and hedonic calculus, promoting the simultaneous embrace of both personal freedom *and* social well-being (Skirbekk and Gilje, 2001: 267). While still certainly remaining an empiricist himself, he advocated including a more qualitative approach to measuring and comparing different states of utility. Furthermore, he argued against the presiding *laissez-faire* economic policy of the time, believing it naïve to assume that any interference with markets was coercive and detrimental to the (typically middle-class) individual's freedoms and happiness and thereby negative. He believed free trade was *not* a natural state of affairs and, fearing the "tyranny of the majority" (Stromberg, 1981: 108), felt it was the responsibility of government to intervene for the benefit of *all* through protective legal reforms (Skirbekk and Gilje, 2001: 269). His theoretical foundation was then still an "individualistic capitalism," but one that was flexible enough to "entertain exceptions to the rule whenever a sound case could be made" (Stromberg, 1981: 107), a list that grew steadily as he matured. He would certainly have supported the contemporaneous industrialist Robert Owen's objections to "competitive individualism and perpetual demand for increased productivity," and his attempts at New Lanark to harmonize productivity and employee well-being (Duncan, 2007: 89).

John Stuart Mill, indicative of this evolved species of deliberately socialized utilitarianism, was evidently more quintessentially humanist than those who preceded him, in that he believed, without reservation, in the "spiritual nobility" of personal freedom, to the extent of attempting to protect every individual, as far as reasonably possible, from the freedom of others to infringe upon one's basic inalienable rights. Ultimately he sustained that the goal and purpose of any civilization, indeed the *only* end really worth striving for, were: "the complete development of the individual's powers to the highest possible point" (Stromberg, 1981: 108), a notion not altogether removed from the ideas of early Greek thinkers, and indeed, as discussed in Chapter 4, those made famous by the clinical psychologist Abraham Maslow, a little under a century later.

Historians repeat each other, history repeats itself

> [A] creature of a very particular time.
>
> (Hutton, 1996: 27)

The effective oscillation between individualist and collectivist political ideals witnessed in Britain in the nineteenth century (and in the philosophical debates of the pre-modern and medieval eras) has remained an enduring pattern in contemporary social and governmental debate. Accordingly, Barley and Kunda conceive that popular discourses do not evolve in a progressive, linear fashion but tend rather to alternate periodically, between prominent underlying ideologies of "normative or rational control" (1992: 304). With the alternating emergence of each "trend" (ibid.) being a reaction to the cultural dearth of the previous, occurring when the myths upon which each are based are no longer popularly sustainable (recall Herzberg, 1972: 24).

They propose these ideological vacillations are identifiable across five temporal periods between the American Civil War (1861–1865) up until the early 1990s, when their argument was published, outlining initially "Industrial Betterment" from approximately 1870 to 1900, in which, as detailed above, the "normative" ideas of John Stuart Mill and Robert Owen were embraced by a "generation of reformers" as part of a movement to "alter industrial conditions" and facilitate co-operation and employee welfare (Barley and Kunda, 1992: 304). This was, however, superseded by the ensuing age of Scientific Management, between roughly 1900 and 1923, which ushered in and was defined by a highly rationalized approach to work and societal arrangement. As discussed at greater length in Chapter 3, this set of popularized ideas was then later displaced by the Human Relations movement, a return to normative methods of organization and control between circa 1923 and 1955, only to be succeeded itself by the functionalist Systems Rationalism trend from the mid-1950s to early 1980s. At which point, the more normative era under the managerialist administrations of Thatcher and Reagan and known as the Organizational Culture movement, emerged.

Welfare capitalism

While segmenting history in such a fashion can appear reductive, it does help to highlight trends for the purpose of analysis. Barley and Kunda's argument is introduced then in order to delineate their third "normative" Human Relations epoch, from the early 1920s to the mid-1950s, a period synonymous politically with "welfare capitalism." The sociological theory of the welfare state emerged out of "great historical convulsions and crises": from the background of the capitalist Industrial Revolution and the emergence of a politically organized and enfranchised mass of wage earners, but especially from recovering battle-wearied populations in the aftermath of the Second World War demanding significant change and new guarantees of safety in peacetime from their governments (Naschold, 1994: 9). It was hence a phenomenon not localized to any one particular country, but rather a general enacted agreement across Western democracies with their populations that the machinery of the state should: provide economic security, equality and social rights and services for all of its citizens; facilitate a substantial redistribution of resources from the wealthy to the poor; and be "explicitly responsible for the basic well-being of all its members" (Kaufman, 1985: 45). This again recalls the *non*-individualistic and communally-based beliefs of Plato and Socrates concerning the "ideal state," (re-)establishing concern for the individual and their personal happiness as a collective and societally mediated issue.

   After the official cessation of world hostilities in 1945, corporate North America manifested such endeavors "almost overnight" in efforts to harness human "loyalty, motivation and satisfaction" rather than purely scientized regimentation (Barley and Kunda, 1992: 314). These philosophies were developed in influential institutions, including: the New York State School of Industrial and Labor

Relations at Cornell, the Yale Labor-Management Center, and the Institution of Labor and Industrial Relations at the University of Illinois, who, as (supposedly) politically neutral bodies, were "charged with institutionalizing a system of collective bargaining" (ibid.). Consulting firms and business schools likewise offered expertise in areas of industrial relations, organizational and work redesign, focusing specifically on the "human side of enterprise" (ibid.).

The welfare state in Britain, which reportedly gave the movement its name (Goodin and Dryzek, 1987: 46), also enacted dramatic and long-lasting changes to the social and political landscape. The Conservative Party's victorious war-premier Winston Churchill was succeeded by Clement Attlee's Labour Government on 26 July 1945 (although Churchill was returned to office in the following election on 26 October 1951). Attlee embarked on a series of "cradle to grave" welfare state reforms, resulting in: the creation of the National Health Service; the nationalization of major public utilities, such as the Bank of England and the coal, steel, gas, electricity, telephone and railway industries to ensure their fair allocation; and benefit and pension reforms. Social security was also reconsidered so as no longer to benefit only the dependent labor force, but also to incorporate the self-employed and unemployed (Flora, 1985: 19). Furthermore, a number of landmark pieces of social welfare legislation were passed: the Family Allowances Act of 1945; the National Assistance and National Insurance Acts of 1948, and the Housing Act of 1949, in addition to the introduction of cheap meals and free milk for school children, immunization and the expansion of hospital services, the abolition of means testing for social payments, assistance to evacuees and "aid to those suffering damage to life, limb or property as a result of the war (under the War Damages Act of 1941)" (Goodin and Dryzek, 1987: 47).

Of particular importance was the extension of the scope of coverage of the state's benevolence and care to its *entire* population. In Britain particularly, prior to the war, most programmes had been aimed at the indigent, but with the technological and tactical warfare developments such as the deliberate bombings of civilians, attempts to enforce starvation through naval blockades and the creation and use of nuclear weapons, a much greater proportion of citizens perceived themselves to be directly at risk. This "pervasive uncertainty" hence "changed people—their beliefs, attitudes, expectations and values—in a way that the First World War (absent mass bombings etc.) did not" (ibid.: 67). The preceding mythic dogmas of Anglo-American society had hence begun to "hurt people too much" (recall Herzberg, 1972: 20), culminating in the widespread, multi-nation expansion of collective moral rather than personal-hedonic horizons. This was perpetrated through socio-political channels towards a humanist programme of facilitating well-being and happiness through parity, provision and the protection of society, rather than the purposeful enablement of the individual: a result which would likely have been received well by, among others, John Stuart Mill.

It would, however, be remiss to suggest that the post-war welfare state and its approach to the construction of the "good society" enjoyed universal consensus. Since its inception, it has endured numerous critics, many of whom warned that it was a step back along the road to "serf-dom and economic ruin" (Mishra, 1984: 1). Observers of corporate life in particular admonished that the cost of cohesive organizations and societies was the loss of individualism resulting in a "homogenized mediocrity," and limitations on firms' abilities to respond to changing market conditions (Barley and Kunda, 1992: 315). However, for some 40 years, "outside a small circle of faithful anti-collectivists" such critical ideas made limited political and intellectual headway. While Social Democratic and Conservative Parties across Europe and North America may have differed greatly on specific matters of policy and their enactment, both "more or less hugged the middle ground" throughout this period, maintaining an essentially socialistic conceptualization of society and citizenry (Mishra, 1984: 1).

The "modern" turn

This was until the 1980s, however; the beginning of Barley and Kunda's fourth "rational" ideological surge, when heightening disillusionment with the power and performance of the welfare state came to a crescendo. Concern about the world-wide fiscal crises of the mid-1970s helped mark the end of the negotiated consensus on its necessity (Walker, 1994: 185), as the "entire paraphernalia of compulsory social insurance, as well as state programmes of health, education and housing" came to be seen as belonging to another age of austerity, privation, unemployment and the absence of economic growth (Mishra, 1984: 2). The tangible increase in personal riches for many now meant that "the wasteful and unnecessary 'universality'

of indiscriminate state provision" could be replaced as a culturally palatable foundational myth system, with a liberalist return to
individualism and "selective provision for the genuinely needy and
poor" (ibid.). A number of Anglo-American welfare state initiatives in
particular were thus discontinued or reversed after the Conservative
Margaret Thatcher assumed the Premiership: "when [she] became
prime minister of Britain in 1979, and then Ronald Reagan President
of the United States in 1980, it was clear that the economic era
inspired by New Deal ideas and policies had come to an end" (Bakan,
2004: 21).

As discussed in Chapter One, Thatcher's prized mandate was to
reverse the legacy of state involvement and economic decline left
to her by the previous Labour Prime Minister, James Callaghan. She
embraced a hard-line approach to terror, war, political prisoners,
crime, trade unions and the unemployed; all for what she envisioned
to be the *greater good* of the nation and its citizens. Acutely reducing state intervention with markets, she was a proud advocate of
entrepreneurialism and sold off many nationalized utilities to private
firms, assuring the populace that competition would necessarily lead
to an improvement in service. Furthermore, many council tenants
were offered the right to buy houses from local government, in a bid
to (re)instil self-determination, responsibility and "rampant individualism" (Hutton, 1996: 28) very much in the heart of British society.

These changes would have arguably suited the original liberalists
and utilitarians of Bentham's era. It was a dramatic return to *laissez-
faire* and the atomistic and hedonistic appeal of the maximum
freedom of individual entrepreneurs from government regulation
and opposition to factory legislation and trade unions that defined
the first half of the eighteenth century (Stromberg, 1981: 65,109),
in an economic philosophy dubbed *neo*-liberalism. In an interview
with the tabloid magazine *Women's Own*, Thatcher outlined her
position:

I think we've been through a period where too many people
have been given to understand that if they have a problem, it's
the government's job to cope with it. "I have a problem, I'll get a
grant". "I'm homeless, the government must house me". They're
casting their problem on society. And, you know, there is no such
thing as society. There are individual men and women, and there

are families. And no government can do anything except through people, and people must look to themselves first.

(Thatcher in interview with Douglas Keay, 1987)

This denouncement of the notion of "society" strikes resoundingly with Bentham's rejection of all "conceptual terms" that hold social reality as anything other than the collation of individuals seeking to maximize their own individual happiness; and a number of commentators have indeed concurred that the pragmatic and individualistic breed of utilitarianism has again become the social and economic basis of contemporary Anglo-American civilization (cf. Hutton, 1996; Gray, 2002; Thrift, 2005b; Ferguson, 2006). Prosperity and happiness were then (once more) deemed to be best sought legitimately by self-motivated individuals, aided by such acts being sanctified in legislation: "[the present] growing fashionability [of utility] in the United States is a cultural product of a country that enshrined the right to happiness in its 1776 Declaration of Independence" (Fineman, 2006 308; cf. Layard, 2005: 5).

Frank Furedi summarizes this Zeitgeist and the particular formulation of utilitarian thinking currently (back) in fruition:

> The celebration of happiness as a virtue in and of itself is motivated by a powerful mood of atomisation and disenchantment with public life. Western societies attach less and less value to those virtues and emotions that demand social engagement and civic responsibility. Emotions aimed at self-fulfilment tend to be presented positively, while feelings that bind the individual to others are regarded with suspicion ...Today's emphasis on feeling good reflects the fact that the individual self has become the central focus of social, moral and cultural life.
>
> (Furedi, 2006a)

As already postulated, central to the present embodiment of *neo*-liberal, hedonistic and Utilitarian fiscal and social philosophy is that, if left unfettered, economic markets will naturally find a point of equilibrium, which will enable those sufficiently motivated to make of their lives what they will, leading directly to increased happiness for some and indirectly for the remains through the "trickledown" effect of wealth. Thus those who are able to amass money will spend it, fueling the economy and ultimately benefiting all. This is why trade unions, wage councils and worker legislation were attacked both in the early 1800s and under Thatcher's and Reagan's regimes, as they were seen as unnatural hindrances to this process (cf. Hutton, 1996).

However, Ehrenreich points out that such a perspective holds a particular, convenient affinity with society's "economic winners", namely those who occupy powerful and high-paying jobs, as it helps explain and justify their success in personally flattering terms while invalidating any potential complaints of the "losers" (2006: 85). This recalls Sklair's comment in the previous chapter that *neo*-liberalism retains a *self-justifying rhetoric* designed to persuade others of its innate fairness (1995: 98–9), and Hill's description of capitalism acting to convince those "who wished to be convinced" (1996: 40, cited in Scott, 1998: 119). If relative success, well-being and happiness are judged primarily in terms of individuals, those who are *un*happy can be explained away as either anomalous or not having made sufficient efforts to be otherwise.

This then becomes a self-sustaining prophecy as it promotes the message: "It's not the world that needs changing ... it's *you*," and there is no need to "band together to work for a saner economy or even to band together at all" (Ehrenreich, 2006: 85, emphasis in original). Hutton concurs, stating that in *McKinseyland*, his nod to the influential power of management consultants (recall Saint-Martin's reference to a *Consultocracy*, 2000: 20): "we must look to [people], government and regulation for the sources of productivity weakness, not to the way the markets themselves are functioning" (Hutton, 2002: 228). Individualist, managerialist *neo*-liberalism hence rejects (as did Seneca) notions that circumstance or environment can be considered responsible for one's position in and approach to life, compared to individual will.

Hutton informs then that there is "no constitutionally protected conception of the public interest that exists independently" of what the governing bodies of a society desire (1996: 35). It is rather determined by which discourses or myths are held in high regard by a society at any particular historical juncture, which presently have resulted in the popularization of the *Homo happicus* subject position. As posited previously, it is of course possible for citizens to comport themselves in any manner of being, but there is a significant discursive pressure for it to be in accordance with that pursuant to the politico-economic mainstream imbued by such institutions, and their composite actors, objects and templates. The contemporary ambition to individualize and "marketize" "every aspect of the way we live," is thus argued to have eroded the overtly social dynamic of life, which Hutton states actually weakened the economy (ibid.: 192). The contemporary *neo-liberalist*, utilitarian ideal of *greater happiness for the greatest number* through free markets and trade, sanctification of the entrepreneurial spirit and individual hedonic pursuit of one's own agenda is then conceivable as: "a curious ... archaic ... relic of Enlightenment rationalism" (Gray, 2002: 198); and, as will be explored, perhaps an endeavor to chase "a Utopia that can never be realized" (ibid.: 2).

The political need for happiness

> Every paradise is a paradise lost.
> (Proust, cited in Duncan, 2007: 95)

It is now necessary to ascertain whether the contemporary historically recurring embodiment of individualistic, utilitarian political-economy is able to increase the generic happiness of a population; or if there is a fundamental problem with attempting to manipulate it at a macro-governmental scale. It was the opinion of many of Bentham's critics that any scientistic, economistic and individualist approach is destined to fail, as such a prerogative cannot eliminate inequality, and in fact thrives on it, which surely renders it unable to provide widespread happiness. Similarly to Schopenhauer, Freud also considered individual's happiness in society as an impossibility, as the inevitable restrictions placed upon one's primal and instinctual needs (those that would satisfy the *id*) would necessarily prevent its fruition, wherein "civilized man has exchanged a portion of his possibilities of happiness for a portion of security" (Freud, cited in Duncan, 2007: 91). The uninterrupted happiness of every individual within a society is thereby unsustainable, as at innumerable junctures it would entail one individual's infringing upon that of another—the bane of John Stuart Mill's life. Happiness, for Freud, is then the expression of instinctive, uncivilized desires (so in trying to be happy we, ironically, may actually unleash something quite unpleasant), and all that any society can hope for is to negotiate a workable compromise between communal safety and personal satisfaction.

Duncan thus provides a line of argument with which to prom-
ulgate that the current, concerted political endeavor to orches-
trate societal happiness is unlikely to succeed. Returning to his
oppositional "survey-pegs" introduced above, the professed theoriz-
ings of Bentham, Mill and even Thatcher and Reagan, all belong at the
"pragmatic, New-World" end of the spectrum, which Duncan explicates through a discussion of psychoanalytic theory. Considering the
theory of desire as pertinent to understanding happiness, Duncan
adopts a Lacanian view from which desire is perceived to emerge
from our entry at birth into a pre-existing symbolic and discursive
order. While all organisms have a need for certain resources for the
purposes of survival, through speech, humans create an "unbridge-
able gap" between a network of signifiers and these needs. Our ability to ask for things thus renders us in a situation whereby satiable
needs are re-presented as open-ended, non-permanently satiable,
desires (ibid.).

To explicate, Lacan's theory of "lack" advances that "existence and
identity are founded upon a negativity, an illusion of completeness,
focussed upon a *master-signifier*, such as Liberty, Equality, or even
Happiness" (ibid.), the principle being that it is (wrongly) considered
possible for any one such state to be achieved, provided the appropriate constitutive elements can be amassed. However, the process, or
rather circuits, of "new" capitalism manufacture an "ever-widening
field of desire, and innovative ways in which commodities create
invidious distinctions, and hence ever-widening gulfs of resentment,
dissatisfaction and anxiety" (ibid.: 95). General examples could
include the requirements for food and shelter as being fundamental
to the survival of the human being, which are offered to modern
humankind as a near inexhaustible array of possibility, such as
desires for foodstuffs: takeaway, gourmet, healthy eating, fast-food,
vegetarian, vegan, organic, non-genetically modified; or those for
different kinds of domiciles: apartment, bed-sit, bungalow, thatched
cottage, townhouse, family home, second home, retirement complex
(*ad nauseam*).

Thus, the pursuit of happiness sustains the capitalist process as
"it is in the very nature of the desiring subject *not* to satisfy desire"
(ibid., emphasis in original) in any way other than temporarily or
partially, leading to repeat consumption. This could explain the earlier cited news reports that state modern Anglo-American happiness

has not increased in accordance with affluence, as it is moreover the pursuit which is possible rather than the result. While consumers may on average have more disposable income than, say, 50 years ago, with it comes an even greater diversity of open-ended desires upon which to spend it. That which is avoided by the (theoretical) state of happiness: anxiety, loneliness, boredom, sadness, are then actually paradoxically *constitutive* "of Happiness as an ideological fantasy" (ibid.), whereas Utilitarian views would consider them as diametrically opposed; and happiness is a social construction which exists in the human need to promote the potential for escape from these perceived otherly detrimental conditions, rather than being a state which can ever actually be finally and permanently reached:

> Everyone's journey to happiness begins from the same place: unhappiness. We start with the feeling that our lives are out of joint, no matter how stable and fastened they appear … The question …—how do I invest my life with meaning—is a perennial one. Indeed, it is the human question. And behind it lies a general truth about the search for happiness.
>
> (Schoch, 2006: v)

From such a perspective, perhaps Epicurus' oft-criticized suggestion that happiness results rather from the *absence* than the satisfaction of desire has something to it after all.

So why the pursuit?

This psychoanalytic, skeptical, continental, Lacanian or anti-utilitarian perspective, whichever label seems most fitting, outlined above, may be quite compelling from an academic point of view which is free to trade in ideas regardless of their mass appeal. But to the politician attempting to attain or secure power in an age when the political ideologies of personal happiness are so rampant, they are understandably repellent. Very few votes would likely be won by a party publicly expressing that happiness is "mythical" and little can be done to improve it among the electorate. It then becomes clearer why perspectives that seem more pro-active, hailing the "undifferentiated maximization of happiness, posed as a universal human goal that must be supported by government" are more popular, especially when they embrace its "objectivity and universality" (Duncan,

2007: 99). The reality of happiness, and that a political party can provide it, is a very powerful message. It is therefore currently most pragmatic for Anglo-American governments to publicly strive to maximize the happiness of their voting population, or cultural "audience," whether or not it may be theoretically possible:

> Happiness can then serve to justify retrospectively the genesis of liberal-democratic government (that is, "we consented to be governed in the interest of our own well-being") and to justify teleologically our political projects ("the goal of a just government is happiness").
>
> (ibid.)

This political use of happiness as a justificatory mechanism for policies or as a springboard to secure power in the macro-governmental realm renders it then as an ideological and rhetorical concept rather than simply a human feeling. The ambition is to enable the populace to achieve happiness through a prudently regulated lifestyle: "keeping people contented and productive and preventing them from becoming a burden on the taxpayer" (ibid.: 102). On the surface, this makes a great deal of sense, and demonstrates that the current political manifestation of happiness is based on individualist, humanist, rationalist and instrumentalist concerns, and intended to unify personal happiness with organizational productivity and economic development (a relationship discussed further in Chapter 3).

However, aside from the fact that individuals may desire to fulfil the politically sanctioned imperative to *be happy* in manners not in accordance with, say, living healthy, socially aware and productive lives (recall Freud's anxieties on this subject), a more significant conclusion can be drawn. In a democracy especially, any policy designed to maximize happiness will be unavoidably subject to debate, scrutiny or comment by all of the sentient actors detailed in the *Information Generating* and *Audience* sectors of the "Happiness Agenda" (see Figure 1.1). Having said then that happiness has become politicized in modernity, maybe it should rather be argued that, having been appropriated at this level of engagement, happiness in the modern age cannot be *a*political. It is unable to reside outside of rhetoric or political interest when utilized as an agendum or tool of government, either for their own benefit or that of the individuals and organizations under their influence.

Happiness is thus presently pervasive at a macro-political level because of its mythic, utilitarian manifestation, and interest with its pursuit and provision dovetails with the hegemony of *neo*-liberal, hedonic political systems and the operation of the circuits of "new" capitalism. This has resulted in its "unquestionable" (recall Goodchild, 1996: 211, cited in Thrift, 1999: 31) enshrinement in supporting actors, objects and templates, such as political mandates, news stories, scholarly studies and philosophical beliefs. The desire for happiness is consequently reified as being "normal" at a macro-political level, and hence very hard to argue against, and, following the psychoanalytic critique, is even sustained by its relative *un*attainability—for, as felt by Proust, to find one's paradise is to also lose it. Those in positions of relative political authority leading the charge in the pursuit of happiness will then prevail, until the "rivers" of discourse, actants and myths upon which it flows sufficiently shift course, and it is (re)conceived of from an entirely new, collective standpoint.

3
Happiness loves company

> How did the activities of five women engaged in assembling intricate components in a huge Chicago factory come to be seen as representatives of the behavior and aspirations of all workers?
>
> (Gillespie, 1991: 264)

This chapter concerns the second historical shock that contributed to the formation of the modern cultural circuits of happiness: its twentieth-century assimilation with organizational practice, whereby a widespread humanistic belief prevalent in management thinking from this period is that: being happy and productive at work are necessarily connected. This is central to the circulation of the Happiness Agenda as it facilitates its operation at the meso-organizational level of society, bridging between more abstracted macro-philosophical theory and political policy and micro-personal interpretation and enactments.

The aim is thus to address how and why this happy-is-productive belief was formed and some of the mechanisms and actants by which it is maintained within modernity. The first section tracks the origins of this assumption through the history of organizational sociology. It will be positioned as having originated in relation to the development and spread of scientific management, and as being maintained and compounded by the subsequent human relations movement. Elements of its present manifestation will then be discussed in the second section, followed by a discussion providing analysis of *why* it is so strongly felt in society. Finally, the chapter introduces three key multi-realm institutions that have embraced it and the significance of the influential cultural sway they hold. So, in an update of the old adage *misery loves company*, the current cultural trend is rather that *happiness* loves company, or even more appropriately, that *companies love happiness*.

Theoretical origins

> Its specific nature, which is welcomed by capitalism, develops the more perfectly the more bureaucracy is "dehumanized," the more completely it succeeds in eliminating from official business love, hatred and all purely personal, irrational, and emotional elements which escape calculation.
>
> (Weber, cited in Parker, 2002: 19)

There is a strong, widespread belief in contemporary Anglo-American society that the happiness and productivity of human agents, whether employees or citizens, are intimately linked. Numerous organizational theorists have made their reputations by promoting such a view and endorsing ways in which both can be harnessed and effectively utilized. Rather than being a novel discovery, however, the faith in this relationship extends back through history over one hundred years, spanning a variety of theoretical perspectives otherwise often considered incongruent. Despite notable differences and developments in approach, from a particular period of historical inception it can also be shown that there has since presided a common desire among many successive actors dedicated to revolutionizing organizational (and societal) activity, to align the interests of both organizations and the people within them. Such an appetite is based on a unitarist perspective that employer and employee goals *should* be mutual, and instrumentally assumes that corporate and personal ambitions and growth *can* indeed be united with limited resistance, towards individual, institutional and political improvements.

F.W. Taylor's humanity

In his much discussed analysis of the advance of bureaucratic capitalism, Max Weber proffered a fearful admonition. Writing at the turn of the twentieth century, his description, above, conjures images ranging from William Blake's "dark, satanic mills" to Fordist production lines and Tayloristic studies of time-and-motion, mainly reducing the individual to a dehumanized cog in an over-bearing and faceless mechanism, and being restricted to an organizationally desired collection of specific and prescriptive movements. As inferred in Chapter 2, industrial developments in the late nineteenth and early twentieth century heralded a dramatic change from the preceding pervasive work arrangements of "industrial betterment" (cf. Barley and Kunda, 1992) in the United States and Great Britain, as an ethos of rationalization began to radicalize much corporate activity, productivity and aspirations. Increasingly formalized hierarchies of management and bureaucracy were introduced, in search of systematizing and unifying human and organizational processes alike.

Frederick Winslow Taylor is often characterized as the principal harbinger of such bureaucratic trends in the early twentieth century. Although he was arguably rather an individual who has become a figurehead for a fairly diverse group of "systematizers" sharing like-minded intentions at a similar time (cf. Thompson and McHugh, 2002: 29), he "dreamed" of an "ordered, individualized, sanitized, hierarchically differentiated, rational industrial environment" (Taksa, 1995: 440). F.W. Taylor is best known for advocating a prescriptive system for maximizing productivity, whereby the conception and execution of tasks were handled strictly by management and workers discretely; said tasks were broken down into their simplest component movements which were to be followed and repeated most exactly; and only the workers who were best suited physically to the work in question were to be identified and employed.

These concepts of instrumental and rational organization soon met with popular approval, as they very much appeared to "meet the needs of capital in that period" (Thompson and McHugh, 2002: 29), occurring not only at technological and economic levels, but actively reflecting the essence and interests of industrial Western society: "During the [period], the modern [Tayloristic] corporation became a preeminent means of economic organization in America ... [and] when the modern corporation comes into contact with political culture, the causal arrow points simply from the corporate to the cultural" (Miller and O'Leary, 1989: 250). As but one microcosmic example of the receptivity of F.W. Taylor's audiences, Shenhav reports that, in 1881, the New York Public Library held not a single publication on organizational or people management, but by 1910 stocked over 200 (1999: 17, cited in Thomson and McHugh, 2002: 20). Further, F.W. Taylor publicly declared his work as being able to directly address the expressed concerns of President Roosevelt regarding "the conservation of our national resources [being] only preliminary to the larger question of national efficiency" (Taylor, 1947b: 5), gaining much recognition and credibility for his ideas. Also, noted social and organizational reformers, such as Louis Brandeis, were openly sympathetic to the manner in which "scientific management claimed to eliminate arbitrary, socially destructive authority in large-scale organizations" (Miller and O'Leary, 1989: 254).

Significantly, this enhancement and spread of the perceived legitimacy of Tayloristic principles—the adoption of its organizational templates and its embrace by influential actors and instantiation in objects—are reminiscent of the processes by which management consultancy firms were reified to positions of influence over governmental politico-economic policies in the 1980s, as discussed in Chapter 2. While certainly not universal or without critics, the discernible sweeping advent and adoption of a systematic, scientific management in the early 1900s, commonly assigned the sobriquet of "industrial bureaucracy," had a pronounced impact on society, organizations and the individuals within them.

Based on its predicates, it seems hardly surprising that Taylorism is widely considered a machinistic, inhuman system that treats individuals as (inferior) extensions of the production process: "The reduction of scientific management to a series of techniques has now become the dominant orthodoxy in social discourse" (Taksa, 1992: 368), and as indicative of Weber's fears incarnate. However, F.W. Taylor himself stated that while, for example, "the control of the speed problem rests entirely with management" (1947a: 44), his scientific approach was purposefully designed to ensure the mutually beneficial object of both "*high wages* and *low labor* cost" (ibid.: 22, emphasis in original). He even argued in front of a US Congressional committee in 1912 that efficiency should become a shared value of all in the "industrial system," believing it would eradicate conflict between labor and management (Miller and O'Leary, 1989: 255). F.W. Taylor thus recognized and promoted the perspective that the efficiency of the production process was not dependent only on formal control mechanisms, but also on the "informal social features" of the workplace (Taksa, 1992: 367): "The workman should ... be paid a cash premium as a reward for his ingenuity. In this way the true initiative of the workmen is better attained under scientific management" (Taylor, 1947a: 128).

So, rather than the cold characterization so often assumed, F.W. Taylor was perhaps rather relatively humane or indeed, to a degree, (proto-)humanistic:

> [I]t is safe to say that no system or scheme of management should be considered which does not in the long run give satisfaction to both employer and employé [*sic*] which does not make it apparent that their best interests are mutual.
>
> (ibid.: 21)

Rather than malevolently attempting to solidify power in the hands of management through only *technical* means, F.W. Taylor can then be otherwise understood as, first of all, also employing *cultural* control and, second, doing so for the purpose of benefiting all parties involved:

> By restructuring work groups and their relations with supervisory staff in relation to task performance; the elimination of oral modes of communication among workers; the promotion of new recruitment methods; the promotion of new methods of industrial training ... Taylor's philosophy attempted to establish a mode of controlling workplace culture specifically and industrial culture generally.
>
> (Taksa, 1992: 370)

Writing in 1911, Taylor stated that the need for this *unitarist condition* he desired "had not as yet been generally recognized" (1947a: 21–2). He, or rather the ideas he represented, can hence be posed as an approximate historical reference point from which to anchor, relate and compare that which followed. He is certainly not being proposed as the sole actant that led to the practical and mythical developments witnessed, but rather, much like Bentham and the spread of Utilitarianism, as a figure indicative of and who contributed greatly to the emerging political, cultural and organizational environment in which his ideologies were advanced (cf. Miller and O'Leary, 1989: 250).

The human relation

The cultural and mythological developments emerging subsequent to the hegemony of "Taylorism" are commonly described as having radically changed the socio-cultural landscape once again:

> But on the continent of the ego, the response was to be managed in terms of a conception of "human nature" derived from the writings of Abraham Maslow, Carl Rogers, Viktor Frankl, Eric Fromm, and others, one that would allow a translation between the social and cultural values of advanced liberal democracy on the one hand and the demands of industry on the other. In this new image the subjectivity of the individual was conceptualized in terms of motivation, self-direction, and responsibility.
>
> (Rose, 1990: 109)

Despite the (proto-)humanist approach of F.W. Taylor, a subsequent school of thought known as human relations, often regarded as the progeny of Elton Mayo and developing in popularity and influence along with the Harvard Business School, sought to enact further changes by emphasizing to a much greater degree the human agent within the production process. Famously associated with the Hawthorne Experiments, its protagonists considered descriptions and programs for highly rationalized, formally structured and systemically regulated factory conditions as akin to *skeleton outlines*, or "wire reproductions" of motion, that were "quite true" but lacked humanity (Mayo, 1946: 37): "[Researchers] had empirically discovered that one may organize, and apparently scientifically, a carefully contrived enquiry into a human industrial problem and yet failed completely to elucidate the problem in any particular" (ibid.: 53).

Mayo and his contemporaries, perhaps most notably Wallace Donham, the Dean of Harvard from 1919 to 1942, saw themselves as "reformers" endeavoring to ameliorate the inherent "harshness" endemic to Tayloristic modes of industrial capitalism, with Mayo in particular taking considerable effort to position himself as "a moral and political philosopher" (O'Connor, 1999a: 224). Focusing more specifically on the attitudes rather than the actions of workers and employers (Gillespie, 1991: 267), the Human Relations School ultimately sought to reframe the management of culture rather than process to a far more pronounced and primary significance than had been achieved previously.

Ironically, the initial ambition of the Hawthorne Experiments had been to determine which physical and technical factors led to improved production and workplace attitude. However, after far from conclusive results, the very act of focusing on the employees directly became attributed as the causation of the desired positive outcomes experienced. Mayo reported that as an overall result of the battery of experiments conducted at the Western Electric Company there was a marked improvement noticed in employees' attitude towards their work (1946: 74). This generated the conclusion that the simultaneous amelioration in disposition and effectiveness witnessed demonstrated the existence of a causal link between them: "In other words, we could more logically attribute the increase in efficiency to a betterment of morale than to any of the ... alterations made in the course of the experiment" (ibid.). This assumption was seen to be reflected in the recorded opinions of the employees: "comment after comment from the girls indicates that ... they have a feeling that their increased production is in some way related to the distinctly freer, happier, and more pleasant working environment" (ibid.: 77).

As a result, the Hawthorne researchers began to consistently equate higher productivity with human and emotional factors rather than formalized technical direction. This contributed to the prominent, presiding belief that the disciplines of scientific management and human relations were fundamentally different and expressive of a decisive shift or "historical switchover," based on the notion that F.W. Taylor's ideas emanated from "technological integration" while Mayo's directly revolved around "ideological integration" (Taksa, 1992: 382). This is problematic as it relegates F.W. Taylor's already proposed interest in managing culture and, equally, the underlying managerialism of Mayo. For while he spoke a great deal about improving workplace conditions, it was for the overall positive influence this would have for the company, not the workers, in question.

Thus, despite the differing relative interests in the *human* and *technical* elements of production, there is reason to believe that these two perspectives are intimately related. As demonstrated above, Mayo and his co-experimenters viewed the workers as *girls*—"immature, obedient, emotional"—whose satisfaction could be measured simply and axiomatically in terms of their production rates (Gillespie, 1991: 265). The assumption that worker satisfaction and productivity were linked revealed a belief that employees could be measured, as similarly professed by Taylor (and advocates of Benthamite Utilitarianism), and retains the unitarist conception of aligning employer and employee goals towards a greater productive end. Finally, the nature of the language used, assumptions held and styling of the experiments themselves all acted to reflect and maintain the existent hierarchical relations between the supervisors and workers (ibid.). The Hawthorne researchers specifically, and the human relations movement more generally, hence took for granted the complete necessity of managerial control of the workplace (ibid.: 268), echoing Taylor's beliefs regarding the division of the conception and execution of ideas and rationalistic assumptions about human nature which had "characterized Western philosophy since the Renaissance" (O'Connor, 1999a: 224):

> [Human relations] experts and managers reassured themselves that the best administrator, whether a factory manager, army officer, government official, or school principal, was one that could fashion a cohesive group of subordinates who identified with the organization's goals and would spontaneously accept their superior's authority.
>
> (Gillespie, 1991: 268)

Both managerial traditions rest upon similar rational and instrumental assumptions, placing primacy upon the goals of the capitalist enterprise by re-aligning employee action and attitudes to those of the employers, albeit via different methods (Taksa, 1992: 367). In this sense it can be argued that scientific management actually anticipated human relations not only chronologically but ideologically and mythically as well, by "placing upon management the duty of intervening in informal workplace relations" (ibid.: 370), a burden that Mayo *et al.* took up with gusto.

Nevertheless, Taylorist conceptions in the contemporary era are often considered antiquated or outmoded, having fallen from grace in favor of a more overtly humanist outlook. Many work organizations, be they white-collar or blue-collar or even blue-chip, no longer operate in what is considered a classic Taylorist fashion, only interested in an employee "from the neck down" (1947a). While Weber observed capitalist bureaucratization as maintaining a strong affinity with *de*humanization, and the desired, or even required, elimination of irrational and emotional human sentiments, criticisms also commonly levied at F.W. Taylor, the subsequent humanist Zeitgeist has since spawned numerous organizations that actively seek and cater for them. Bureaucracy still exists widespread, numerous organizations employing formal rational techniques can be found, but there is presently a seemingly ever-increasing sway of companies now deliberately also competing for the "hearts and minds" (Parker, 2002: 46) of their organizational members.

A modern-day assumption

> Management consultants, advisors, trainers, personnel officers, and so on, have blazed the way "forward" with their messages proclaiming the "humanization of the workplace", the importance of "self development for productivity", the value of being "yourself at work, the unlocking of human potential" at work.
>
> (Heelas, 2002: 89)

Significantly, such overtly emotion-centric humanistic focus strays somewhat from the original human relations intentions of Mayo, as he was rather more concerned with attending to emotion in order to keep it under regulation, in accordance with "Romantic" (Evans, 2002: xii) or "post-Cartesian" approaches which regarded it as "the very antithesis of one good thing called reason" (Damasio, 1998: 83–4). Indeed, throughout much of the late nineteenth and twentieth centuries, the conceptual and practical integration of the mind and brain, or emotionality and rationality, received widespread disavowal, and emotions were treated as though both too elusive and subjective for the dedicated attention of "concrete" disciplines such as the neuro- and cognitive sciences (ibid.). Even within the sociological realm, emotions had tended to "enjoy a rather ethereal existence," the roots of which were "buried in western thought: a tradition which has sought to divorce body from mind, nature from culture, reason from emotion, and public from private" (Williams and Bendelow, 1998: xv).

Some of the "founders of sociology" did at least "touch upon" emotion with Weber elucidating on "the anxious 'spirit of capitalism'" and questioning the notions of rationality and the magnetic draw of charisma; Durkheim's considerations of the "social scaffolding for feelings of solidarity"; and Marx's explorations in the context of class conflict of alienation, resentment and anger (Hochschild, 1998: 3). Writing in the eighteenth century, even Adam Smith, the founder of the "dismal science" (an epithet for the discipline of economics), also helped to pioneer the "sentimental science" or a "psychology of emotion" (Evans, 2002: xi). However, most sociological theorists retained a segregating perspective, casting emotion and reason as residing at opposing ends of a spectrum. Damasio contends that the "historic neglect of emotion" and its frequent relegation in lieu of rationality, as encapsulated by Utilitarian attempts to secure it in a *felicific calculus*, and a charge against which Mayo could also be considered guilty, had an unequivocal and detrimental effect on understanding as they are the "highest-order direct expressions" in complex organisms and critical for survival (1998: 84). Furthermore, it overlooks the perspective that rational methods of scientific inquiry, "even at their most positivistic, necessarily involve the incorporation of values and emotions" (Williams and Bendelow, 1998: xvi).

As indicated, focus on emotion has recently undergone a renaissance in Anglo-American society: "At the dawn of the twenty first century ... things are rather different. [It] is now a hot topic" (Evans, 2002: xiii). This is also recognized by Bolton who contends: "In the nineties the subjects of love, intimacy and emotion ... entered centre stage of general sociological debate" (2000: 155). It is thus widely believed that, as a cumulative result of the human agents within them, "organizations have feelings," and their "commercialization" is a "common occurrence" (Bolton and Boyd, 2003: 289). One notion in particular which has resultantly gained significant popularity is *emotional intelligence* (EI): "Aristotle's concept of the golden mean is remarkably similar to what psychologists now refer to as "emotional intelligence". [This] involves striking a balance between emotion and reason in which neither is completely in control" (Evans, 2002: 59).

EI is very much orchestrated as an approach and set of techniques by which to facilitate the interplay or "collision" of informal human emotions with formal organizational (be it societal, familial or corporate) structures (cf. Olesen and Bone, 1998: 313). Daniel Goleman, one of the principal architects of the concept, suggests it extends throughout and can be applied and improved in numerous domains, with specific regard to harvesting human emotionality as a significant organizational resource. These include: *knowing* and *managing* one's emotions, whereby enhanced degrees of self-awareness, certainty and appropriateness of feelings are supposedly correlated with the making of improved personal decisions "from whom to marry to what job to take"; *motivating oneself* through the marshalling of emotions in the service of personal goals; and *recognizing* and *handling* emotional states in others, in order to increase "social competence" and leadership, and operate effectively "at callings such as the caring professions, teachings, sales, and management" (Goleman, 1996: 43). He even offers a case study with which to demonstrate the validity of utilizing emotionality within an organizational setting:

Melburn McBroom [an airline pilot] was a domineering boss, with a temper that intimidated those who worked with him ... One day in 1978 McBroom's plane was approaching Portland, Oregon, when he noticed a problem with the landing gear. So McBroom went into a holding pattern, circling the field at a high altitude while he fiddled with the mechanism. As McBroom fiddled with the landing gear, the plane's fuel gauges steadily approached the empty level. But his co-pilots were so fearful of McBroom's wrath that they said nothing, even as disaster loomed. The plane crashed, killing ten people. Today the story of that crash is told as a cautionary tale in the safety training of airline pilots. In 80 percent of airline crashes, pilots make mistakes that could have been prevented, particularly if the crew worked together more harmoniously. Teamwork, open lines of communication, cooperation, listening, and speaking one's mind—rudiments of social intelligence—are now emphasized in training pilots, along with technical prowess.

(ibid.: 148)

Describing the cockpit of an aircraft as a "microcosm of any working organization," Goleman infers how the consequences of problems such as low morale, poor communication and worker intimidation, all of which he contends result from poor emotional management, can be most dire indeed, resulting, if not necessarily in disaster, but at the very least as "a cost to the bottom line" for any company (ibid.). He thus advocates most clearly the benefit or even necessity of positive corporate engagement with human emotionality, as "the single most important element ... is not the average IQ in the academic sense, but rather ... emotional intelligence" (ibid.: 160).

The management and manipulation of employee's feelings are hence presently securely labeled with the notion of competitive advantage (Bolton and Boyd, 2003: 290). Due to the necessarily exploitative nature of this process, Olesen and Bone contend that central to the employment of "emotional intelligence" lies Hochschild's concept of "emotional labor," which empirically and theoretically addresses the cultural, organizational and personal pressures, or templates, enacted upon human agents, to varyingly express or subdue emotions as "deemed appropriate to realize entrepreneurial economic interests" (Olesen and Bone, 1998: 315). Her investigations into "The Managed Heart" highlighted that social actors are able, and often required, to carry out personal emotional manipulation as an integral element of the capitalist labor process (Bolton and Boyd, 2003: 290). As Hochschild outlines: "An act of emotion management [is] to change one's feeling or emotion ...We can – and continually do – try to shape and reshape our feelings to fit [various] cultural guidelines" (1998: 9).

The *neo*-human relation

As a consequence of the organizational embracement of emotionality, employees are being increasingly asked to "unconditionally invest more of themselves" in their work lives (Thompson, 2003: 364). Whereas industrial bureaucracy is commonly considered to have functioned *without* emotion, *post*-bureaucratic organizations are making new demands: "we must ... love our organizations and give our all to them, to operate *with* hatred and passion" (Parker, 2002: 51, emphasis in original); one can then perhaps imagine Bill Hicks resting somewhat uncomfortably in his grave.

This modern trend, symbolic of the perceived "historical switchover" discussed by Taksa (1992: 382) and reminiscent of the advent of "new" capitalism, is very much encapsulated in the publicized opinions of the influential Chartered Institute for Personnel Development (CIPD):

> What became known as "Taylorism", with its emphasis on routine procedures commanded and controlled by an ascending hierarchy of senior, middle and junior managers, was remarkably successful during the "pile it high, sell it cheap" era of standardized mass-manufacturing production. But Taylor's successors in the current generation of management gurus are constantly stressing the limits of scientific management in the knowledge- and service-based and people-centred economies of the early twenty-first century.
>
> (CIPD, 2007: 17)

It can then be sustained that the contemporary managerial advance on human feeling, emotion and sentiment at work is being driven by modern reinterpretations of the human relations movement. Fundamental to this is the unitarist assumption that employee and organizational goals and well-being can be united. This is indicative of the existence today of the belief, predicated on the findings of the Hawthorne researchers, that improving worker happiness leads to increased production. It is thereby widely considered possible to be both humanistic *and* profitable, because treating employees well will make them work harder, a popular notion today that could have been written by Mayo himself.

There is a wealth of literature produced by management writers, consultants and practitioners that supports this contention that a *neo*-human relations assumptive link between productivity and happiness, or even rationalism and humanism, not only exists but is widely prevalent (Gillespie, 1991: 268). For example: the author of *301 Ways to Have Fun at Work*, Leslie Yerkes, suggests: "fun is the single most important trait of a highly effective and successful organization ... in fact, there is a direct link between fun at work and employee creativity, productivity, morale, satisfaction and retention, as well as customer service" (cited in Abner, 1997: 42). Similarly, Helzberg Jr. states that: "associates who enjoy their jobs will share that joy with their customers" (2005: 21); Goldsmith reports: "in companies where people have fun, productivity and profit are higher" (2003: 26); and Ramsey proffers that fun benefits "employees ... and the bottom line" (2001: 7). Emotions such as fun and happiness have then become a very serious business. While the pursuit of the happy/ productive worker might be viewed as an "impossible dream" from a Marxist perspective, or as "too simple or naïve" from a traditional industrial relations view, in more prominent contemporary, popularized psychological and managerial camps, it is very much lauded as a "difficult though worthwhile endeavor" (Staw, 2003: 144).

Staw reports how over the past thirty years there have been a multitude of theories offering to lead managers to the "promised land" of high satisfaction and productivity. These include: *Worker Participation*; *Supportive Leadership*; *9-9 Systems*; *Job Enrichment*; *Behavior Modification*; *Goal Setting*; *The Pursuit of Excellence*, *Socio-Technical Systems*; *Organizational Commitment*; *High Performance Systems*; *Theory Z*; and *Strong Culture* (ibid.: 145).

Each of these influential theories "burst onto the scene with glowing and almost messianic predictions" (ibid.: 144), denoting populist desires to "transform the thinking of the travelling executive" (Grey, 2005: 2). Entering "managerial common sense" (Ledford, 1999: 25) with ease, many were "enthusiastically consumed" (Willmott, 1993: 540) by an array of practitioners eager to both unite humanism with improved performance and conflate company and employee goals. Such desires "clearly owe something to the political, economic and business climate of the 1980s" (Guest, 1990: 377) (as discussed in Chapters 1 and 2) and are indicatory of the "translation" proposed by Rose (1990: 108–9), quoted previously, whereby numerous actants within organizations and society at large are presently acting to negotiate between the requirements of industry and individuals in advanced liberal democracies. They also ratify Gillespie's observation (1991: 264) that the activities of a few employees in a Chicago factory seem to have become considered as representative of all staff behavior writ large.

However, it also demonstrates that despite the "rhetoric of breathless discovery" ingrained in many of the theories identified by Staw, they actually tend to be based on many of the assumptions of the "old" Human Relations School (ibid.: 269), albeit enacted through different mechanisms, which has its antecedents located within the scientific management tradition (cf. Taksa, 1992: 366–7). There was arguably not then a dramatic switch from Taylorism to human relations, or indeed even human relations to more recent modes of human resource management (HRM), defined by Guest as "a set of policies designed to maximise organizational integration, employee commitment, flexibility and quality of work" that act to reduce the impact of collective industrial relations (1987: 503), but rather a continuation of a set of common rational-humanist and instrumentalist myths across differing historical periods. Even Mayo recognized his own work as being an "extension of that begun by the pioneer [F.W. Taylor]" (Mayo, 1924: 258, cited in O'Connor, 1999a: 224). In no small part then thanks to Mayo, the approbation of the "unitarist condition" sought by Taylor (1947a: 21–2) seems very much manifest today.

A misanthropic humanist?

Confirming the views expressed above, O'Connor puts forward that "modern day HRM has indeed remained faithful" to Mayo's core notions "about human beings and what should be done with them" (1999a: 223). As a result, these shall now be discussed in order to further expose the underlying assumptions embedded in contemporary human relations. As indicated, much like the inception of scientific management, at the time of their emergence the Hawthorne experimenters' notions reflected their contemporaneous cultural environment. This was namely a North American, post-war progressivism, a movement articulated at "local, state and federal" levels of American politics that endeavored to "recover a public stake in the conduct of affairs" (Miller and O'Leary, 1989: 253) with the aim of remedying workplace conflicts: "so that workers would be happier and thus not join unions," and combating "fatigue, low productivity and revery'" (ibid.: 236). While Mayo was producing his theories, and Donham was establishing the Harvard Business School, "the world suffered from what historians have called the 'four horsemen of the Apocalypse': the Red scare, influenza, inflation, and industrial strife" (O'Connor, 1999b: 118). With the effects of these conditions and the international economic, political and social devastation wreaked by the First World War, a welcoming receptivity to such ideas emerged.

Significantly, Mayo believed the Great War had demonstrated "man's fundamental rottenness," and that this innate rotten nature required sublimating. As opposed to a sympathetic, moral obligation, he hence aspired to appeal to the *human factor* (namely "feeling" and "irrationality") as he saw emotionality as posing "the foremost danger to civilization" (Mayo, 1919: 16, cited in O'Connor, 1999a: 224).

Rather than a natural human state, for example, he considered *sanity* as an "accomplishment that required training" (ibid.). He conceived of the human being as a bundle of motives, comprising needs, sentiments and drives, not naturally "adjusted" to managerial and organizational imperatives (O'Connor, 1999a: 237). In line with the progressivist spirit of the time, which embodied a belief that "science and experts could solve human problems such as conflict, poverty and crime" (ibid.: 226), Mayo stated with grandeur that his methods would *save civilization* (cf. O'Connor, 1999b: 117), by training, predominantly Harvard, educators in his techniques (O'Connor, 1999a: 227) in order to achieve a state of (internal individual and external organizational) "harmony" (ibid.: 237). Further, evidence demonstrates that these ideas have remained consistently popular:

> Later, Likert (1961) described this state of harmony as "loyalty"; Bakke (1953) as "fusion", McGreggor (1960, 1966) as "identification" and "integration". More recent HRM writers speak remarkably similarly about notions such as "commitment" (e.g. Beer *et al.*, 1985; Storey, 1992), "mutuality" (Walton and Lawrence, 1985), "integration" (e.g. Guest, 1987), and "congruence" (e.g. Beer *et al.*, 1985)
>
> (ibid.: 238)

Such visions saw management becoming reified to the position of "guardian of social order" able to save "humanity from its naturally dire state" (ibid.: 229), and, importantly, also secured as a science. For, if the human agent could be measured, compared and manipulated by workplace initiatives: "this would grant managers the genuine capacity to make people not only do – but also be – what was wanted for the organization" (ibid.) through the formation of idealized subject positions that would appear to suit all involved.

Mayo, the management field's "humanist par excellence" (ibid.: 223), was then indeed, as argued earlier, not so different from his Tayloristic, rationalist, instrumentalist and systematizing predecessors after all, or many of the Utilitarian political reformers discussed previously. One of the main effects of the human relations theories and their subsequent, more recent equivalents listed above, regardless of whether emotions were respectively considered favorably or skeptically, has then been the establishment of an ideological environment in which management and workforce have "positive" relationships, resulting in "well-being" at "individual, organizational and social levels" (Beer *et al.*, 1985: 17, cited in O'Connor, 1999a: 238) – albeit mostly in terms defined by those in positions of relative authority. So HRM, as the contemporary enactment of human relations theory, and an extension of scientific management objectives, holds as integral the unitarist assumption that the happy worker is the productive worker, which despite appearances could be argued as remaining an inherently "instrumental, indeed manipulative, way of appreciating social relations" and emotions (Sayer, 2007: 21), but one that still seems very seductive to governments, organizations and individuals alike. It must now be considered whether this belief actually holds any validity.

Happy workers?

> So long as one is happy one can endure any discipline: it was unhappiness that broke down the habits of work.
>
> (Graham Green, 1975: 34–5)

There is compelling evidence of the "extreme strength" of beliefs in the relationship between happiness and productivity (Fisher, 2003: 757), with both organizational scholars and practitioners having engaged in decades of investigation. However, certain theorists have surmised that little proof actually exists to demonstrate the existence of a strong, evidentiary link. For example, Fisher highlights that "the major" empirical reviews of this correlation, including: Vroom (1964), Petty, McGee and Cavender (1984), Iaffaldano and Muchinsky (1985) and Judge, Thorensen, Bono and Patten (2001) could only demonstrate that: "the average observed [statistically calculated] relationship … is positive but relatively weak, in all cases between 0.14 and 0.25" (Fisher, 2003: 754).

Fisher then provides explanations as to why so many studies may have failed to prove something widely considered to be common knowledge, believing that: "a better understanding of the theoretical basis for expecting or not expecting a relationship to exist is needed" (1980: 607). For researchers attempting to objectively prove the existence of a relationship already considered apparent may fail to take account of the possibility that it simply is not. Furthermore, fundamental problems result from attempting to discover a relationship between an *attitude* and a *behavior*. Fisher feels then that there is presently a distinct lack of consistency among researchers' conceptions of whether an individual's attitude or behavior is best considered at either one instance or as an aggregated general pattern that accounts for variation, leading to an incongruence and incompatibility between different studies.

Finally, Fisher relates the need to address scales of attitude, differentiating between, as example, "patrons' attitudes to *their own* church rather than *the* church," and also varying behavioral criteria: "like church attendance or monetary contributions" (ibid.: 607–10, emphasis in original). She concludes that while the relationship between job satisfaction and performance seems to have intrinsic appeal and value, those who study it should "understand in advance the [problematical] type of relationship they are seeking—one between a *general* attitude and a *specific* behavior" (ibid.: 611, emphasis added), and take steps to establish a consistent methodology that can at least account for some of the issues she raises.

Beyond the array of methodological research problems outlined, there still remains a need to address why perceptions of the happy-is-productive worker are so strong, despite the lack of correlating evidence. The journalist-cum-writer Polly Toynbee (referencing a government-funded ESRC Future of Work Programme) suggests rather than a nation of content and efficient workers: "nearly half [of British employees] work more than their basic forty-hour week, with 81 per cent working long hours not because they enjoy it but because they need the money" (2003: 109). Similarly, the Work Foundation, previously known as the Industrial Society, records that: "job satisfaction has plummeted over the last decade" (ibid.). There is thus much to contradict the authenticity of the happiness–productivity assumption, and the validity of the initiatives it spawns, but little appears to be decisively impacting its embrace. The next section addresses why this may be so.

The need to believe

The human relations-inspired happiness/productivity axiom (or *controversy* according to Petty *et al.*, 1984: 712) is indicative of two core beliefs: that the "two variables *should* be related and, as a result, further research will reveal the as-yet-undiscovered truth" (Iaffaldano and Muchinsky, 1985: 268, emphasis added). This correlates with the concerns and desires of a rationalist and instrumentalist culture, to which a contrary conclusion that the two entities are only slightly related (as the evidence actually infers) would likely be most troubling: "The ideals of high job satisfaction and high productivity are valued in our society, and attempts to design work so as to jointly achieve these goals are continuous" (ibid.). Such an environment begins to help explain the prominence of the assumed relationship despite the lack of evidence, but further understanding can still be gleamed from the related literature.

Fisher offers an analysis that complements her previous work from 1980, expanding again on technical research issues that may explain why the "self-sustaining myth" remains (2003: 772). She allows that "lay people" might observe or experience a strong relationship between happiness and productivity "at a higher or lower level of analysis, or at a longer or shorter time span, than that usually investigated by scholars" (ibid.: 757). Further, their personal definitions of "satisfied" or "happy," for example, may be incongruent with those of researchers (ibid.: 760). These are fair points and the self-reflexive awareness that subjects of investigation can know themselves differently than an external observer is indeed beneficial for research. Yet the term "lay people" occurs in her work quite often and is used as a handle for *anyone who is not a social scientist*, which itself could be considered slightly problematic. For, paradoxically, while outlining the various methodological problems researchers can face, she is actually creating another by segregating academic research from any external *real* world, as though it is a distinct and different place "out there" awaiting discovery by better equipped non-lay persons such as herself. This is an artificial and non-beneficial distinction, and ironically recalls elements of both the assumptions outlined by Iaffaldano and Muchinsky (1985: 268) above.

Moving on from Fisher's *technical* explanations, Ledford (1999) offers a *cultural* analysis as to the promulgation of the happy-is-productive "myth." Rather than focusing on why the relationship may be difficult to prove, he considers why so many practitioners (both individual and managerial) *want* to believe in it. Advising that the correlation is often only assumed to be strong "until examined more closely," he proposes an elementary thought experiment:

> Think of the times in which you have been most happy. Perhaps you were newly in love, hit a lottery jackpot, or witnessed the

birth of a child. I see no evidence that our happiest moments tend to be our most productive.

(ibid.: 26)

He feels that if such a simple demonstration can shake the cogency of this assumption so ingrained in modern-day human relations, which looks increasingly "suspicious the more we inspect it, [then] something interesting is happening" (ibid.). Referring to researchers, Ledford theorizes that there is a presiding *aesthetic* encouragement to accept the happiness–performance connection as it is "elegant, neat and inclusive": the field has shown a preference for "theories that explain both performance outcomes such as productivity, quality, and customer service, as well as attitudinal outcomes such as job satisfaction" (ibid.: 28). He hence suggests we may "fool ourselves" into accepting a theoretical proposition "that explains too much" (ibid.: 30) due to the pleasing appeal of its simplicity and applicability, recalling the assertion in Chapter 1 that management consultancy products are popular as they are packaged as functional and simplistic tools (cf. Thrift, 2005c: 36; Fincham and Clark, 2002: 1).

Ledford also traces the happy-is-productive assumption (through Barley and Kunda, 1992) to the dawn of the Industrial Revolution in the United States, showing that it "gained prominence through the Industrial Betterment movement that began in about 1870" (Ledford, 1999: 26). As contended previously, at this time influential figures argued that societal and organizational benefits would stem from utilitarian investment in the social infrastructure of schools, housing, libraries and recreational facilities for employees and their families. Prominent contemporaneous British examples might include the towns of Bourneville, created by Cadbury's and New Lanark, established around cotton mills by Robert Owen, mentioned in Chapter 2, both purpose-built to house and care for the respective companies' employees. This prevalent, culturally maintained myth then received another surge of support in the 1920s from the human relations movement which, as already discussed, continued promoting the need for establishing constructive social relationships for the purposes of improved organizational effectiveness (ibid.). Ledford thus proffers that employees have historical precedence *and* ideological reasons to believe in this thesis: by accepting it, any requests for improved facilities, pay and conditions can be legitimated against the return in productivity that will be offered in exchange to management (ibid.: 27). Each party then has a vested interest in actively and jointly believing in the existence and validity of a correlation.

Hollway (1991: 265) also offers an interesting, complementary insight both into the emergence of human relations and the focus on satisfy-ing the employee as a worthwhile endeavor. In light of the complex discursive inter-relations between power, knowledge and practice, she propounds that students, teachers and practitioners are often ignorant of the historical context of ideas, as so much emphasis seems to be placed rather on scientific knowledge, and its promise of positive, pro-gressive reform. Rather than believing that an attitudinal-behavioral relationship already exists and merely requires finding, she argues that "like in other applied social sciences," it has, recalling the criticisms of Fisher, been *produced rather than discovered* (ibid.).

By focusing on its social construction, a justifiable approach based on the lack of evidence and yet strong appeal, it is possible then to raise questions about the conditions of its production: "about the situations in which problems are defined, by whom, with whose interests incorporated" (ibid.). Gillespie can be called on to substan-tiate this approach as he urges that "science is an inherently social activity" (1991: 266), rendering the conception of a purely objective, *a*social science fundamentally misguided, as "all knowledge will bear the imprint of the social context in which they are constructed" (ibid.: 267; cf. Williams and Bendelow, 1998: xvi). Accordingly, Hollway (1991: 268) sees "virtually no" debate regarding the status of the knowledge that supports much of human relations, resulting in a situation whereby the discipline is often uncritically assumed to be rational and non-partisan., a belief that contributes to the wide-spread acceptance of its theories and notion that the attitude and behavior in question *must* be related:

> Motivation and job satisfaction are not phenomena that exist in some universal and timeless state that awaited human relations science to discover and apply them. Both the concepts and the practices that confer on them some kind of material reality are a product of changes in the organization of work, which were themselves the result of the dominance of some interests over

others; of owners (both private capitalists and the state) over laborers.

(ibid.)

Substantiating Ledford's argument above, and the previously contended notion that such theories both result from and reflect the contemporaneous social, political and economic environment, Hollway infers that the problem of motivating a workforce resulted from a general societal and organizational need (recalling the essence of Roosevelt's speech) to create sufficient satisfaction in order to produce adequate work (ibid.): "Facts are not discovered during experiments. Rather experimentation is one of the resources that can be mobilized by scientists to establish a fact" (Gillespie, 1991: 266). The emergence of this belief was thus not merely a moral, humanistic concern, nor a neutral, natural and rationally discovered development occurring in isolation from its protagonists, but arguably rather a practical means to a particular temporally and culturally determined end. This contributes to an understanding of why the "possibly naïve but compelling logic" (Fisher, 2003: 772) of the happy-is-productive worker has become so ingrained in modernity, and is often defended so vigorously despite a lack of clear, corollary proof.

Champions of the new human relations

> Whatever the complex reasons for Maggie and Wilma staying in that kitchen, it certainly had nothing to do with loyalty to ServiceTeam whom they detested, along with the catering managers' insufferable exhortatory messages pencilled at the bottom of our rota ...with a hand-drawn smiley face and a sad face, with the words, "Always Happy, Never Sad!"
>
> (Toynbee, 2003: 110)

The preceding sections of this chapter argue that due to mythical and practical developments in the twentieth century, a network of prominent organizational actants collectively embraced the prevalent politicized notion of the provision and utilization of happiness from within a human relations movement framework. In accordance with abounding utilitarian ideals, such institutions acted to promote a rationalist, instrumentalist and humanistic agenda, embracing the unitaristic happy-is-productive worker hypothesis. This was then (re)interpreted in order to suit more modern organizational and societal needs, arguably projecting and promoting the preferred cultural subject position for corporate citizens of a purposefully employed *Homo Happicus*.

In addition to the legion of complicit institutions, a number that require specific attention occupy an interesting social and cultural space, located and operating across the macro-, meso- and micro-sociological realms. One is the CIPD, introduced above, and the others are two related academic movements, the *Positive Organizational Scholarship* (POS) and *Positive Organizational Behavior* (POB). Recalling Rose's identification of the humanist *translation* presently occurring between the cultural values of society and requirements of industry, POS, POB (and the CIPD) could be regarded as the vanguard of this shift: "Positiveness [*sic*] is a recent strand in organizational theorizing, focusing on understanding the "best" of the human condition" (Fineman, 2006: 270). According to some of its proponents, it is a "new movement," dedicated to the human dynamics that lead to "exceptional individual performance" (Cameron and Caza, 2004: 1).

POS thus assumes that "every day" human and organizational behavior usually fails to reach its full potential, (ibid.: 3) and endeavors to redress this by developing techniques to measure, improve or instil *strength, vitality* and *flourishing* in employees (Bernstein, 2006: 266). Other "HRM interventions" favored by these positivity scholars include:

> Empowerment programs to "vitalize" and "positively energize" organizations, shifting employees toward greater positive commitment to organizational goals (Collins, 1993; Deal & Kennedy, 1999; Feldman & Khardemian, 2003; Meyer & Allen, 1997); programs to boost emotional intelligence (Cherniss, 2001; Dulewicz & Higgs, 2004); and programs aimed at increasing positiveness through "fun events" at work (Weinstein, 1997).
>
> (Fineman, 2006: 277)

On the official POS website (www.bus.umich.edu/positive/) there is a Mission Statement in which it is declared that two of the key activities of the movement are to "develop and market POS educational cases and tools," and "disseminate" POS ideas and intellectual products to "scholars, students, corporations, nonprofits, and communities" (www.bus.umich.edu/Positive/Center-for-POS/Mission. htm). There are also several links to webpages outlining other institutions to which POS is connected. These include: not-for-profit organizations such as *The Positive Futures Network, Business as an Agent of World Benefit* and *Building Great Places to Work* (www.bus. umich.edu/Positive/POS-Research/Related-Not-for-Profit-Orgs.html); funding bodies: namely, *The Fetzer Institute, The Gallup Organization* and *The Templeton Foundation* (recurring in the following chapter) (www.bus.umich.edu/ Positive/POS-Research/Related-Funding-Orgs. htm); and related research groups, the most noteworthy of which is the *Positive Psychology Center* (also featuring in Chapter 4) (ibid.). This demonstrates the potent reach of the POS group, the cultural actants, or "weaponry" (recall Thrift, 2005h: 137), under its command, and the degree to which they are sympathetic to the human relations myths previously explicated regarding how the human agent should be conceived of and managed within organizations.

Similarly to POS, POB is described as: "the study of and application of positively oriented human resource strengths and psychology capacities that can be measured, developed and effectively managed for performance improvement in today's workplace" (Luthans, cited in Roberts, 2006: 293). This resonates as a modern interpretation of Mayo's earlier cited desires for "citizens to be measured, compared and manipulated" (O'Connor, 1999a: 299) into *doing* and *being* what is wanted by the company. To compound such a contention, Luthans and Youssef published a paper – with the subtitle "Investing in People for Competitive Advantage" – in which they advocate organizational concern in employee "self-efficacy, confidence, hope, optimism and resiliency" (Luthans and Youssef, 2004). This demonstrates the combining of rationalist, instrumentalist and humanist thinking, and how it is becoming manifest in the effective contemporary translation between social and organizational needs (recall Rose, 1990: 109). POB is thus an actor able to present management researchers and practitioners with objects and behavioral templates focusing on a "potential source of competitive advantage to explore and on which to capitalize" (Luthans and Youssef, 2007: 334), and doing so from a very influential platform.

Finally, the CIPD also has an official website in which they describe themselves as a "professional body for those involved in the management and development of people" (www.cipd.co.uk). Their influence is felt throughout many companies, not least in the recruitment process, to the point where finding any job in (British) human relations departments is now becoming increasingly difficult for graduates who do not have independent CIPD qualifications and accreditation. It has over 125,000 members (www.cipd.co.uk/about) and every month a quarter of a million hits are made on the website (www.cipd.co.uk/about/areport/careerbuilding.htm). As an organized and formally recognized body, one of their principal aims is to impact upon public policy by liaising with government and civil servants: "We use our research and members' professional experience to develop pragmatic, rather than political, views. This often means explaining the practical effects of adopting one particular method rather than another" (www.cipd.co.uk/about/publicp.html).

Many of these "pragmatic" views concern the managing of emotion, well-being and happiness at work: "Without this knowledge ... organizations place themselves at a serious disadvantage whether in terms of managing individual performance, reducing absence or retaining and recruiting staff" (www.cipd.co.uk/CMSTraining/Psychology+of+Management/Psychology+of+Management/PWB.htm). The CIPD, along with POS and POB, therefore exert a convincing degree of influence, being able to establish, reinforce, promote and disseminate their complicit actants across macro-political, meso-organizational and micro-personal realms.

The neo-humanistic focus represented by POS, POB and the CIPD (in addition to the myriad compliant companies throughout Anglo-American society) clearly reflects the popular promotion of the unitarist assumption that by addressing the social and emotional needs of employees, organizations and society in general will directly benefit. Recalling the implicitly seductive nature of such a belief, despite the afore-mentioned lack of compelling evidence, it is fairly easy to see why such groups have marked appeal and are becoming very influential in the realms of contemporary organizational activity. In light of the above, O'Connor's statement that "HRM has not really much new in it...but this reincarnation of old ideas is not recognized" (1999a: 238) seems quite acute—especially when considering F.W. Taylor's (often ignored) legacy. A rationalist-humanist approach and the happy-productive worker assumption have then become accepted as a *moral agenda* and justification for focusing on "positiveness" (Fineman, 2006: 270), happiness and well-being at work; and how doing so can provide a: "fix, or antidote, to the malaise of twenty-first-century" organizational life (ibid.). Polly Toynbee's quote used to open this section reflects, however, one example of the managerial adoption of this principle not necessarily leading to the outcomes commonly expected.

The politicized utilitarian translation of happiness discussed in Chapter 2 can then be argued as having drip-fed from the philosophical realm into a sympathetic, receptive and similarly configured organizational climate marked by the rational and instrumental theories of human relations, which has acted to operationalize it in managerial and institutional practice, thereby comprising the primary connections between the first and second formative ideological *shocks* that have contributed substantially to the engineering of the circuits of happiness. This has led to the production of templates for subject positions and a self-promoting and self-sustaining internal consistency and (re)validation across the two sociological levels, the macro- and the meso-, via the mimetic interactions between numerous supporting actors and objects in the *extraordinary discursive network* of research groups and their publications, companies and their policies, academics and their theories, management consultancies and the recommendations and laypersons and their assumptions, who likewise sustain that the link between being happy *and* productive is a tenable, worthy and moral pursuit. Happiness is thus integral to how modern Anglo-Americans be and see themselves in both political and organizational terms, emanating from Enlightenment, utilitarian, and human relations-inspired vocabularies that have conspired, or aligned, to produce our contemporary reality. Attention now turns in Chapter 4 to why, how and where it is also increasingly infiltrating the sociological micro-level of individual practice to complete the circuit.

4
Positively happy

> Our popular culture, and now – owing to the domi-
> nant, separatist Message [sic] of some spokesper-
> sons for the positive psychology movement – our
> professional culture are saturated with the view that
> we must think positive thoughts, we must cultivate
> positive emotions and attitudes, and we must play
> to our strengths to be happy, healthy and wise.
>
> (Held, 2004: 12)

This chapter details the third shock to have transpired, enabling happiness to become central to and circulate throughout modernity: the
(predominantly) twenty-first-century emergence of a practicable *positivity* within influential psychological circles and society at large. It is
affective at a micro-sociological level, supporting the meso-human relations and macro-utilitarian developments previously discussed and, in
addition to the prominence of *Positive Organizational Scholarship* (POS)
and *Positive Organizational Behavior* (POB), derives most notably from
the formalized *positive psychology* movement.

   This ideological development is a major "force of identity" on the
"map of where counts" (recall Thrift, 1999: 52) in the Happiness Agenda,
as it significantly reinforces the Anglo-American cultural embracement
of individualistic subject positions and templates that promote a
hedonistic, rationalist focus on one's personal happiness. Thus, the first
section introduces the emergent discipline of positive psychology, the
second outlines its core foundational principles and relation to happiness, and the third addresses its historical and conceptual origins in

humanistic psychology. Finally, the chapter concludes that the, somewhat incongruent, mythic foundations of the discipline may have actually contributed to, rather than hindered, the widespread acceptance of positivity, and thereby happiness, in contemporary society.

The Manhattan Project

> Psychology, you would think, is a pretty serious and pretty complicated undertaking. Given the importance of its aims and implications, the complexity of its subject matter, and the moral and philosophical intricacies involved in the study of a species by itself, one might expect to find on entering its territory an intellectual structure at least as complex and imposing as nuclear physics ...What one does encounter, however, is more like a bazaar.
>
> (Smail, 1993: 13)

Positive psychology has a number of champions, but of them all it certainly cannot be considered without due and initial reference to its influential founder, Martin Seligman. In 1996, he was elected president of the prestigious American Psychological Association (APA) by the widest margin in its history. Two years later he delivered an address heralding his formalized attempt to "enlarge the scope" of psychology's work by focusing directly on making the lives of people *better* (Seligman, 1999) and *lastingly happier* (Seligman *et al.*, 2004: 1379). The idea struck him, he admitted, while gardening with his 5-year-old granddaughter, who told him that as she had decided to stop whining it was only fair that he should accordingly "stop being such a grouch" (Seligman, 2005: 3–4).

The vehicle he advocated with which to achieve these goals was to be: "A reoriented science that emphasized the understanding and building of the most positive qualities of an individual: optimism, courage, work ethic, future-mindedness, interpersonal skill, the capacity for pleasure and insight, and social responsibility" (Seligman, 1999). Significantly, Seligman stresses the social and historical necessity of focusing on *what makes life worth living* as a tonic to the exponential increase in the number of cases of clinical depression, arguing the illness has multiplied tenfold in Anglo-American

society since the 1960s in a time of otherwise unprecedented economic prosperity. In congruence with the afore-cited "evidence"
from the BBC and Reuters in Chapter 2, he believes this represents
the major paradox of modern life, and that: "no medication or
technique of therapy holds as much promise for serving as a buffer
against mental illness as does human strength" (ibid.; cf. Seligman,
2005: 3; Keyes and Lopez, 2005: 45).

A "new science of human strengths," a deliberately *positive* psychology, which Seligman compares to The Manhattan Project due to
its "unprecedented promise" (1999), had thus been born. One that
could "articulate a vision of the good life" and demonstrate which
actions would lead to "wellbeing, positive individuals, flourishing
communities and a just society" (ibid.). From its onset then, while
emanating from the mind-sets and actions of the individual, the
effects of positive psychology were intended to apply across the
varied inter-connected realms of the socio-cultural spectrum, by:
"Ideally ... document[ing] what kind of families result in the healthi-
est children, what work environments support the greatest satisfaction among workers, and what policies result in the strongest civic
commitment" (ibid.).

Similarly, the discipline's official website (www.ppc.sas.upenn.
edu/index.html), part of the University of Pennsylvania's homepage,
where Seligman is currently Director of the Positive Psychology
Center, describes itself as supporting: families and schools that allow
children to flourish; programs of civic engagement; and therapists
who nurture patients' strengths rather than identifying weaknesses.
There is even a link to Penn State's "Authentic Happiness" webpage,
which boasts circa 700,000 registered users, offering several "scientifically tested happiness questionnaires, surveys and scales" (www.
authentichappiness.sas.upenn.edu/).

Seligman has been most active in garnering financial, political and
scholarly allies for his ideas, describing in his APA address a number
of networking projects as being "under way" (1999). One he determined worthy of specific reference is a collaboration forged with
the Templeton Foundation, creating the annual *Templeton Positive
Psychology Prize*, an incentive scheme for researchers working in the
field, comprising the largest monetary reward ever given in psychology. Coincidentally, Dawkins, referred to earlier, describes, in his *The God
Delusion* of 2006, the Templeton Foundation as an organization that

tends to heavily remunerate scientists who are primarily "prepared to say something nice about *religion*" (2006: 19, emphasis added).

From its inception, Seligman's progeny has then generated a substantial degree of interest and reaction. It has entered mainstream as well as scholarly and political discussion, and was even a focus of the BBC2 documentary series entitled *The Happiness Formula* (aired in Britain between 3/5/2006 and 7/6/2006). In an integral interview, Seligman conveys the benefits of positive psychology as increasing positive emotion, engagement and happiness: "People actually might be physically healthier, they might even live longer, and they might do better in their jobs" (Easton, 2006b). The narrator then supplements, informing viewers: "In the same way that traditional psychology takes a depressed person and makes them less depressed, positive psychologists take a happy person and make them even happier" (ibid.).

Within the positivity literature, causal associations between positive experiences, emotions and happiness and receiving longevity and good health are recurrent themes, referred to by Held with slight sarcasm as being a "trump card" (2004: 20). One case in particular is reiterated by a number of Seligman's supporters. Described by Fredrickson (2003: 330) (and also found in Layard, 2005: 23 and Gable and Haidt, 2005: 107), it concerns a retroactive study conducted on personal essays written by young Catholic nuns in the 1930s. Sixty years later the writings were analyzed by psychologists from the University of Kentucky as part of a study on Alzheimer's disease, and were scored for positive emotional content, recording instances of happiness, interest, love and hope. They reported that the nuns who expressed the most positive emotions "lived up to 10 years longer than those who expressed the fewest" (Fredrickson, 2003: 330). A similar study is shown by Layard regarding actors who have won an Academy Award, in which he demonstrates axiomatically that Oscar winners live on average four years longer than nominees who lose (2005: 24).

The fundamental "rules" of positive psychology, as delivered by voiceover in the BBC2 documentary, are therefore recounted as being easy to follow: a better life will result from the acts of "challenging negative thoughts, playing to your strengths, seeking out meaning in your life and counting your blessings" (Easton, 2006b). Limited highbrow knowledge (unlike for Plato) or weighty financial investment is seemingly required, resulting in an array of actionable, pragmatic techniques, ideas and mind frames with broad appeal. Smail's opening comment that psychology is typically a complicated, serious undertaking (1993: 13) seems then somewhat undermined by the functional and directly applicable nature of this new school of thought to the life of the layperson, as it most ingeniously appears to have found a way by which to translate the intricacies involved in a "species studying itself" (ibid.) into a digestible, widely accessible format.

Principles of positivity

> To the positive in all of us ...
> (Snyder and Lopez, 2005a: dedication)

In March 2003, a special conpendium edition of the journal *The Psychologist* was published, dedicated to the exposition of positive psychology. It provides a unique framework with which to assess the core concepts, beliefs and assumptions, and from which other complementary publications can be incorporated. The journal will thus be used is this manner due to its wide-ranging contributions, covering its varied rhizomatic encroachments into other subjects as diverse as politics, public policy, economics, organizational activity and the private lives of individuals.

The journal in question is entitled *In a positive light* and the front cover is dominated by a picture of a lighthouse besieged by stormy seas, waves breaking on the rocks at its foot, and shining a light out that culminates in a yellow, round smiling face overlooking the maelstrom below. The image is that of a *smiley*, a simplistic representation of a grinning face, primarily used to denote happiness. The deliberate use of a smiley on the cover of this special edition journal, presumably intended to portray pictorially positive psychology as a beacon of enlightenment or counsel through trouble and adversity, is of more than passing interest. As the Introduction to the journal, written by the guest editors, states in clear and no uncertain terms that "positive psychology is about happiness" (Linley *et al.*, 2003: 126). It then opens with a short article by Seligman, in which he outlines certain rudimentary principles, taking notable effort to confirm Linley *et al.*'s proposition, that: "*Happiness and well-being are the desired outcomes of positive psychology"* (Seligman, 2003: 127, emphasis in original).

A negative imbalance

Seligman initially provides a brief historical overview, situating positive psychology as a harbinger of dramatic change to the general paradigmatic emphasis previously adopted by psychology over the past half-century. While offering relative praise, he believes that psychologists have so far focused overly on the singular narrative of mental illness: "After 50 years and 30 billion dollars of research, psychologists and psychiatrists can boast that we are now able to make troubled people less miserable, and that is surely a significant scientific achievement" (Seligman *et al.*, 2004: 1379).

He hence suggests that while sterling progress has indeed been made, it has alas come "at a high cost" (Seligman, 2003: 126). This cost is that while the discipline has centered upon identifying and alleviating states that make life miserable, any antipodal study has been neglected and relegated: "we largely forgot about everyday well-being" (Seligman *et al.*, 2004: 1379), a notion echoing sentiments of his APA address. Such views are also voiced by a number of other writers, including: Chesney *et al.* who argue that increased research on "the positive hemisphere in the global world of emotional life" would yield enhanced better physical health and prevention of disease (2005: 51) (recall the previous examples given of long-living nuns and actors); Maddux, in reference to clinical psychology, who argues that a prevailing illness rather than wellness "ideology" is held firm by many clinicians (2005: 13, 15); Fredrickson in his discussion of a similar propensity in the field of the study of emotions (2003: 330); and Smail (albeit arguing a different point), reporting: "The notion that there is something 'wrong' with the person in distress which has to be put 'right' is absolutely central to the medical and psychological disciplines which have grown up over the past 150 years" (1993: 19).

Western thought is thus suffused, states Seligman (2003: 126), with 'rotten-to-the-core' conceptions of humanity—recall in Chapter 3 Mayo decrying humanity's "fundamental rottenness" (1919: 16, cited in O'Connor, 1999a: 226)—as encapsulated by the prominent Catholic religious doctrine of man being born into *original sin*, and Freud's secular view of humankind engaging constantly in a battle with his/her base sexuality and aggression. From such a pervasive perspective, he argues, it is widely considered that virtuous human action always overlays a very malign nature; and it is this "doctrine" that positive psychology was specifically created in order to over-throw: "more plausible is the dual aspect theory that the strengths and the virtues are just as basic to human nature as the negative traits" (Seligman, 2003: 127; cf. Seligman, 2005: 3). This negative predilection, and the possible positive alternative, are encapsulated quite poignantly in the following excerpt from the Preface of the *Handbook of Positive Psychology*:

> Imagine a planet where the inhabitants are self-absorbed, hopeless and filled with psychological problems and weaknesses. Confusion, anxiety, fear and hostility race through their minds. These creatures "communicate" with each other by lying, faking, torturing, fighting and killing. They hurt each other and they hurt themselves. Of course this imaginary planet is not far away – we call it Earth …
>
> Now let us imagine another planet where the inhabitants are caring, hopeful and boundless in their psychological strengths. Their thoughts and feelings are clear, focused and tranquil. These creatures communicate by spending time talking and listening to each other and to themselves. Again, this imaginary, not-so-far-away planet is Earth.
>
> (Snyder and Lopez, 2005a: ix–x)

Gable and Haidt (2005) concur, offering explanation for this historic one-sided preoccupation with negativity. First is *compassion*: an innate need in humanity to help those who are suffering before those who are already doing well (ibid.: 105); second is the *pragmatic and historical* pressure: as after the Second World War funding agencies tended to prioritize bankrolling research on mental illness to help returning veterans (ibid.: 106; cf. Seligman, 2005: 3; Seligman *et al.*, 2004: 1379); and finally, it results from *evolutionary survival* mechanisms: because humans are hardwired to recognize and attend to potential threats more readily than potential rewards (ibid.; cf. Seligman, 2005: 7; Wright and Lopez 2005: 31). Similarly, Fredrickson believes that this imbalance results from negative emotions generally being harder to differentiate and study, as, first, positive emotions are often "universally" expressed with a *Duchenne smile*, and, second, the array of negativity available is much vaster: "scientific taxonomies of basic emotions typically identify one positive emotion for every three or four negative emotions" (2003: 330–1).

Positive psychologists hence clearly propose an approach that advocates *duality* in the conception of human agency and motivation, composed of the benign *and* the malign, yet which concentrates its efforts towards highlighting the positive aspects, in order to redress the "philosophical, historical and theoretical" imbalance identified (Gable and Haidt, 2005: 107). Accordingly, adopting a Utilitarian approach, Seligman *et al.* contend in "A balanced psychology and a full life" that while for the approximate 30 percent of Americans who suffer a severe mental disorder an "excellent job of helping" has been done, the remaining majority now need to be attended to, as the "absence of maladies does not necessarily constitute happiness" (2004: 1379).

A positive terminology

Having argued for a re-balance of psychology, in the second half of his article in *The Psychologist* Seligman outlines a terminology upon which a "scientifically viable positive psychology might rest" (2003: 127). Initially, three types of "desirable life" are distinguished: the *pleasant*, the *good* and the *meaningful*. In discussing the first of these, "positive emotions" are divided into three categories: "those directed towards the *past* (e.g. satisfaction, contentment, pride, serenity), the *future* (e.g. optimism, hope, confidence, trust, faith) or the *present*" (ibid., emphasis in original). Those concerning the present are then subdivided into *pleasures* and *gratifications*. Pleasures are also sub-classified as being either *bodily*, "momentary positive emotions that come through the senses," such as: tastes, smells or sexual feelings; or as *higher*, those that are also momentary, but more "complicated" and "learned," including: "ecstasy, rapture, thrill, bliss … [and] relaxation" (ibid.). Seligman accepts and states very clearly that pleasures of the present, as well as positive emotions about the past and future, are in effect *subjective*, explaining his aim as being to provide a system within which they can be identified as being "stable" and "consistent" in essence, and then discussed. He thus envisages the *pleasant life* as that which "successfully pursues the positive emotions about the present, past and future" (ibid.).

Alternatively, the *good life* is one concerned more with securing an abundance of gratifications, which, as opposed to the moral philosophy of hedonism, are not feelings like the pleasures but activities: "reading, rock-climbing, dancing, good conversation, volleyball, or playing bridge, for example" (ibid.). Gratifications are all-consuming, blocking an awareness of present emotion, which can then only be felt in retrospect: "Wow, that was fun!" (ibid.). The final category, the *meaningful life*, includes one further element to that of the good life: "*the use of your strengths and virtues in the service of something much larger than you are*" (ibid.: 127, emphasis in original). In pursuit of *meaning*, it becomes "our life task to deploy our strengths and virtues in the major realms of living: work, love, parenting" (ibid.). Such an existence is marked by a connection, to another person, group, organization or a system of belief, which has a bearing and consequence beyond an individual's own existential condition.

While, of course, some classifications and generalizations must be made in order to discuss anything, and bearing in mind Hendrick and Hendrick's caution that "we should not dismiss a concept because we do not currently know how to measure it" (2005: 475), the overall desire and attempt here by Seligman to create such a lexicon, in addition to certainly being a humanistic endeavor, smack very much of a rationalist mindset. Furthermore, his expressed belief that subjective emotions are amenable to rigorous scientific enquiry, classification and, generalized comparison correlates his work with the classificatory and measurement schema of Bentham's *calculus of felicity* (recall Stromberg, 1981: 68), discussed in Chapter 2.

Gable and Haidt (2005) contribute to such terminology by arguing that the purpose of their discipline is to facilitate the *flourishing* or *optimal functioning* of people, groups and institutions (ibid.: 103). This tellingly reveals an inherent assumption held by the authors, or at least implicit in the language they have chosen, that human agents are generally not operating at their maximum capacities (similar to the views held by POS and the Human Relations School presented in Chapter 3), implying they can be enhanced as so to reach a pinnacle of optimality or efficiency, much like an automated production line, and that all other activity can be measured against it: "Psychology was said to be learning how to bring people from negative eight to zero but that's not as good as understanding how people rise from zero to positive eight" (Gable and Haidt, 2005: 103).

This further belies an instrumentalist belief that there are patterns in positive human activity that can be studied, replicated and prescribed, and correlates with Seligman's opinion that "subjective" pleasures and emotions are both "stable" and amenable to scientific study (2003: 127). Further, by labeling normality as point zero, associated ascending and descending scales become definitionally implicit. That which is normal is hence subjugated to that occurring within the superior potential range by the very language used to describe it, rather than necessarily in relation to any actual physical or emotional activity.

Such a discursive process occurs organically when human agency is considered as though akin to a temperature gauge—an assumption made explicitly by Layard (2005: 12). For if you assume you can measure a base point of normalcy, and downwards into depression, you must then logically be able to also measure upwards toward human flourishing. This is a specific interpretation of the concepts of happiness and human agency, which is then sustained and reinforced by subsequent, supplementary work of fellow positive psychologists, elevating the positive in life from something which merely *is*, to something which *should* and *can* be. Taylor argues a similar line, connoting: "positive in the most general sense has no externally verifiable objective standard … it only means how it is defined by those who presume to have the greatest control over how it is defined" (2001: 16). As testimony, Gable and Haidt detail the generation of numerous edited volumes, handbooks, conferences, university and high school courses, grants and researcher collaborations focused on positivity throughout the world (2005: 103). Describing it as a *movement* (ibid.: 105), they hence offer a rallying call-to-arms for potential supporters: "If … you agree that our field is better off with an understanding of flourishing to complement our understanding of despair, then you too may be a positive psychologist" (ibid.: 104).

This implies that the discipline can welcome a whole variety of theorists, appealing to potential supporters at a base level of common sense as well as academic argument. One such convert was Fredrickson—winner of the Templeton Positive Psychology Prize in 2000 (Held, 2004: 21)—who describes herself as having been *drawn* to the discipline from her background in studying emotions (Frederickson, 2003: 330). Such ideas seem then to have grasped the Zeitgeist of the contemporary age: "the time was right for a correction and an organized positive psychology movement" (Gable and Haidt, 2005: 107). Alternatively, however, it could also be postulated that rather than merely emerging within and complementing a swathe of myths, actants and ideologies currently dominant throughout modernity, as with utilitarianism and human relations, positive psychology is a major "pole of innovation" (recall Thrift, 1999: 52) in league with them and one of the major players in the cultural circuits of discourse on happiness, being a major cause in itself rather than merely an effect.

Positively utilitarian

Returning to *The Psychologist*, the second article by Veenhoven (the main architect of the Rotterdam World Database of Happiness) argues that governmental public policy: "could—and should—be aimed at advancing" the "fundamental emotion" of happiness within society (2003b: 128). This clearly reaffirms that which the journal editors and Seligman have already outlined as positive psychology's desired outcome and, additionally, furthers the status and degree of influence its aficionados presume to exert upon individual members of the public and governmental and organizational policy, reminiscent of Utilitarian lobbyists and the defining element of Seligman's *meaningful life*.

Veenhoven reminds his readers that Bentham defined happiness as the sum of pleasures and pains and as "the overall appreciation of one's life as a whole" (ibid.). This recalls the afore-mentioned notion of the duality of human agency, as happiness is posed as an amalgam state resulting from consideration of both the positive and negative factors in one's life, addressing the rebalance called for. Thus, as happiness from this perspective is viewed as a cumulative personal evaluation (cf. Diener *et al.*,2005: 63), it can then supposedly be quantified by simply asking people about it: "It is an overall judgement; so it can be measured by single questions" (Veenhoven, 2003b: 128).

Veenhoven then attests most clearly that it is possible to engineer increased happiness for a population across political, organizational and personal realms:

At the *macro* level, happiness depends heavily on societal qualities such as wealth, justice and freedom. Social policies can improve these conditions. At the *meso* level, happiness depends on institutional qualities, like autonomy at work or care in institutions. Organizational reform can improve such situations. At the *micro* level, happiness depends on personal capabilities like efficacy, independence and social skills. Education and therapy can improve these proficiencies.

(ibid.: 128–9, emphasis in original)

This denotes an underlying opinion that happiness derives from specific, identifiable sources, and can be instrumentally manipulated by measures such as enacting *social* and *organizational reform*, or by *improving education*. The above indicates then that Veenhoven supports the particular conceptualization of happiness that correlates with the mythic underpinnings of modernity and the utilitarian and human relations vocabularies explicated previously.

Bretherton and Ørner then provide an engaging article in *The Psychologist* series, headed by an image of another smiley, draped in a Grim Reaper cloak and holding aloft a scythe. In it they highlight what they consider to be a striking congruence between positive psychology and "therapeutic approaches derived from existential philosophy" (2003: 136). While existentialism, they argue, is typically associated with "personal confrontations with misery, hardship and death," the main aim of this branch of therapy is to clarify and elaborate the patient's way of being-in-the-world: "This is what makes the existential perspective a positive approach—it seeks to examine and illuminate what is there, rather than correct what is lacking" (ibid.).

This is similar to Seligman's advocacy of positive traits being basic to human nature (2003: 127). As Bretherton and Ørner continue by asserting that the most "obvious parallel" between the two schools of thought is that for each there is a preoccupation with "what is presented by the client rather than global models of deficit and disorder" (2003: 136). While existential psychotherapy and positive psychology may have clearly different, opposing and polarized origins, they do both appear to have certain conceptual similarities. Most conspicuously, that the individual is deemed more significant than their environment, in that the focus is on altering their *relational* "way of being in the world," rather than viewing them as an isolated being who can attempt, successfully or otherwise, to alter the world itself.

The penultimate article in this special issue journal thus enquires: *How much do external factors affect well-being?* In it, Oswald offers the reader a system by which the effects of *personal* (such as health, income and marital relations) and *external* (like inflation rates or the vicinity of airport flight paths) factors can be judged in order of relative importance and then acted upon: "It requires us to weigh up different influences on well-being, and put values on one thing compared with another. Economists like me have recently developed a way to do just this" (Oswald, 2003: 140). This correlates with Seligman, Parks and Steen's promise that: "science can illuminate components of happiness and investigate empirically what builds [them]" (2004: 1380); and with Diener, Lucas and Oishi who proclaim: "researchers have succeeded in developing scientific methods for studying subjective well-being" (2005: 64). It also recalls Veenhoven's claim—as shared by Seligman (2003) and Gable and Haidt (2005)—that *happiness can be measured by single questions* (2003b:128).

Positivity in practice

Positive psychology is then argued to influence and enhance a range of worthy fields. In addition to that already discussed, one further example is that of child psychology, where an emphasis on models of individuals "adjusting, adapting and accommodating" to troubling events or illnesses is favored over the more typical, negative coping and resilience methods (Roberts *et al*, 2005: 663). Similarly, the discipline can reportedly help in the *defining and fostering of successful ageing*, by providing interventions that enable "elders to shift from problem-focused to emotion-focused coping mechanisms" (Williamson, 2005: 676, 681), and facilitate "positive growth" following acquired physical disability (Elliott *et al.*, 2005). Notably, each of these examples recall Bretherton and Ørner's (2003) individualist analysis of positive psychology's advocacy of affecting an agent's "relational way of being" in the world, rather than campaigning to alter the world itself.

The discipline is thus a potent, valid and serious force, capable of assimilating a wide range of other factions of psychology within its areas of interest. This is indeed one of its specific aims, as demonstrated by the example of Gable and Haidt offering a "call-to-arms" (2005: 104), rather than merely a possible consequence: "if all goes well positive psychology may not be around for much longer" (ibid.: 104). The discipline endeavors to become sufficiently mainstream as to eclipse *psychology*, so that a discrete title will no longer be needed: "When it is no longer necessary to make distinctions between 'positive psychology' and 'psychology as usual', the field as a whole will be more representative of the human experience" (Seligman *et al.*, 2004: 1381).

A paradigmatic shift is hence called for towards: more positive diagnosis (cf. Maddux, 2005); positive personal action (Seligman, 1999: 126–7); positive organizational behavior (cf. Turner *et al.*, 2005); and even a system of positive ethics (cf. Handelsman *et al.*, 2005). This will enable, argue Snyder and Lopez in their *Declaration of Independence*, the field to address both philosophical questions (such as "what is the good life?") and practical issues ("how do we achieve the good life?") in unison (2005b: 751), demonstrating the discipline's prominent affect at the level of the individual, and the ability of its actors, objects and templates to circulate throughout related organizational and political realms.

In the Foreword to the *Handbook of Positive Psychology*, Sir John Templeton, founder of the Templeton Foundation referred to previously, thus describes the field as developing a "more wholesome" approach, led by "courageous," "visionary leaders," gathering information about the "many gifts that God has given to each and every human being" (in Snyder and Lopez, 2005a: vii). While Templeton's comments and religious views cannot necessarily be extrapolated to all of those who have contributed to the field—bearing in mind the financial support Seligman has encouraged him to provide—it is significant that they should open the weighty tome that represents one of the obligatory points of passage to the discipline, as the *personal pursuit of spiritual principles* he refers to arguably resonates aptly with the overall endeavors of positive psychology.

As with any organized school of thought, positive psychology has then a set of foundational assumptions and beliefs that effectively unites its field. Fineman characterizes these under the term *positive deviance*: the "movement's rhetorical and moral/ideological stand" (2006: 271). While virtually no discipline is entirely homogenized, the concepts that principally underlie its ontological and mythological ways of thinking can still be thought of as being relatively uniform. For positive psychology they can be summarized, based on the preceding literature review as: a substantial argument for the re-balance of psychology, to enable the humanistic focus on "what makes life worth living" (cf. Seligman, 1999: 126–7); such states, traits and emotions are, despite being subjective, sufficiently "stable" as to be amenable to a process of scientific enquiry (cf. Seligman,

2003: 127), which is to be conducted through empirically robust and rationalist measurement (cf. Seligman *et al.*, 2004: 1380), for the purposes of comparison and classification (cf. Seligman, 2003: 127) and creation of a "replicable, cumulative, and objective science" (Held, 2004: 27); this will result instrumentally in improved physical health (Ryff and Singer, 2005), happier lives (cf. Seligman *et al.*, 2004: 1379), better, more productive work organizations (cf. Henry, 2003; Hill, 2003; Luthans and Youssef, 2007: 332), increased civic engagement, and therefore an improved society overall (Seligman, 1999: 126–7), which should facilitate for a large number of individuals the active pursuit of a *meaningful life* (cf. Seligman, 2003: 127).

However, most significantly, while meaningful engagement with others in the forms of family, groups, organizations, politics or a higher power, is certainly strongly advocated, to achieve these ends, one must alter, adapt, or improve their own way of relating to the world through various interventions, driven by the self. The human agent is thus the responsible agent and primary focus; reminiscent of both Thatcher's and Bentham's dismissal of "conceptual terms" such as *society*. Positive psychology likewise encourages, through political, media and scholarly discourse, all who will listen to internalize its conceptualizations, leading to a happiness revolution emanating from within the individual.

Historical and conceptual origins

> We would hasten to emphasize that this positive psychology perspective is not a brand new one. Indeed pioneering thinkers over the past several decades have provided compelling exemplars of positive psychology in their theories and research endeavors.
>
> (Snyder and Lopez, 2005b: 752)

Having positioned positive psychology as an influential and dynamic entity within contemporary society, this next section now demonstrates where it itself has emerged from. As, following the methodological mandate of establishing a genealogical *history of the present*, it is arguable that few thoughts can ever be entirely novel, but must in some way be based on or influenced by a rhizomatic network of previous incarnations. Snyder and Lopez, authors of the above opening epigraph, refer to Seligman's 1998 APA address as the "watershed" point (ibid.) in their movement's history. Yet they are also quick to deny that it was an entirely new way of thinking that was ushered in, but rather, as with Bentham, F.W. Taylor and Mayo, a decisive point from which a conglomeration of concerned individuals already theorizing and working in a likeness could become coordinated. This is echoed by Gable and Haidt (2005: 104), who describe it as having a long history, dating back to William James' writing in 1903 on "healthy mindedness," Allport's (1958) interest in positive human characteristics and Maslow's advocacy of "the study of healthy people in lieu of the sick" in 1968.

Martin thus reports that: "as a movement, positive psychology is still in its infancy ... although it is reclaiming much research retroactively" (2007: 89). Similarly, Mahoney asserts: "[while] the term *positive psychology* is of recent coinage, it shares a rich legacy with humanism, health psychology, constructivism, and spiritual studies" (2005: 745, emphasis added). Resnick, Warmoth and Serlin expand on this connection to humanism specifically by inferring that the movement clearly echoes themes of humanistic psychology from the past three decades, in particular, the work of two other APA presidents, Carl Rogers and Abraham Maslow (Resnick *et al.*, 2001: 74). They even somewhat contradict Mahoney's contention that the discipline's name is of *recent coinage*, by revealing that the final chapter of Maslow's *Motivation and Personality* (first published in 1954), is entitled "Toward a Positive Psychology" (ibid.: 75).

A humanist history

Since the Cartesian conceptual split of mind and body in the seventeenth century, there have been a catalog of remedying attempts to reunite the two entities as a holistic and complete, albeit complex, whole. One such twentieth-century concern became known as the *organismic* viewpoint, and while this word has since fallen from popular discourse, a number of prominent theorists came to fruition under it; it is now more commonly regarded as the *humanistic* movement. Organismic theory primarily emphasized that unity, integration and organization are the natural state of the normal personality, while "disorganization is pathological, usually brought about by an oppressive or threatening environment" (Hall and Lindzey, 1960: 296).

The organism is assumed to be motivated by the "sovereign" drives of *self-actualization* and *realization*, meaning: "that man strives continuously to realise his inherent potentialities by whatever avenues are open to him" (ibid.: 298). Goldstein, a major contributor and proclaimed originator of the term "self-actualization" (if we ignore St Thomas Aquinas, recall Skirbekk and Gilje, 2001: 125), considered the goal of a normal, healthy, person to be not simply to discharge tension but rather to equalize it, resulting in a "centering of the organism" (reminiscent of Mayo's notion of *harmony*, discussed in Chapter 3); however, "full centering or complete balance is an ideal holistic state and is probably rarely achieved" (ibid.: 303–4). The individual is not considered a "closed system" yet the impacts of external, environmental factors are minimized, stressing rather that which is internal and innate: "A normal, healthy organism is one in which the tendency towards self-actualization is acting from within, and overcomes the disturbance arising from the clash with the world, not out of anxiety but out of joy of conquest" (Goldstein, cited in Hall and Lindzey, 1960: 306).

Abraham Maslow, regarded as the "father of humanistic psychology" in both pop-culture (cf. www.wikipedia.org/wiki/Abraham_Maslow) and academic circles (cf. Maslow, 1998: 3), aligned himself very closely with the organismic point of view, using the term "self-actualization" frequently in his book *Motivation and Personality* (1970). Significantly, he lambasted psychology for its "pessimistic, negative and limited conception" of humankind and for studying sins to the neglect of virtues (Hall and Lindzey, 1960: 325): "Where is the psychology ... that takes account of gaiety, exuberance, love, and well-being to the same extent that it deals with misery, conflict, shame, and hostility?" (Maslow, cited in Hall and Lindzey, 1960: 325). He considered this of importance as he assumed humanity to have: "an inborn nature which is essentially good, and is never evil" (ibid.: 326). In direct contrast to the prevailing cultural "rotten-to-the-core" conceptions (recall Seligman, 2003: 126), he desired ultimately to "vastly improve life" (Maslow, 1970: 164). He also admitted to adapting Goldstein's theory of self-actualization (Resnick *et al.*, 2001: 46) in order to produce a: "more complete and comprehensive science of the human person" (Hall and Lindzey, 1960: 327).

Another similar-minded humanist was Gordon Allport—one of the three to whom Hall and Lindzey's *Theories of Personality* is dedicated—who also emphasized the positive, conscious elements of human motivation (ibid.: 260). He too saw marked discontinuity between normal and abnormal behavior, advocating the benign rather than malign: "Theories such as psychoanalysis may be highly effective as representations of disordered or abnormal behavior; however, they are of little utility in any attempt to account for normal behavior" (ibid.). Significantly, he wished to understand how psychological method and findings could be applied in an "action setting," to ameliorate undesirable social conditions. However, he opposed both "extensive borrowing from the natural sciences" and "a premature emphasis" upon the importance of *operationism*: a detailed concern for specifying the "measurement operations implied by each empirical concept," fearing it would serve to impede progress (ibid.).

Thus, Maslow contended that humanistic psychology had opened the doors to study "the psychological phenomena which can be called transcendent or transpersonal, data which were closed off in principle by the inherent philosophical limitations of behaviorism and Freudianism" (1970: xxvii). These limitations concern rationalist and empiricist metatheoretical assumptions, as while "most of the best minds in psychology were pushing relentlessly toward increasing rigor and quantification," the humanists "serenely pursued [their] own way, advocating the importance of the *qualitative* study of the individual case" (Hall and Lindzey, 1960: 257, emphasis added). Allport, especially, held a "distrust of the customary analytic techniques" (ibid.) adopted from the physical sciences or behaviorist approaches, being very critical of mechanical models (ibid.: 260). In order to realize the "organismic goal of studying the whole person" (ibid.: 330), an over-emphasis on quantitative methods of analysis was disavowed:

> The investigator may choose to study behavior in terms of general principles, universal variables, and a large number of subjects (nomothetic); or he may elect to focus on the individual case, using methods and variables that are adequate to the individuality of each person (idiographic) ... the individual or idiographic approach is eventually the more desirable and will lead to better prediction and understanding.
>
> (ibid.: 277–8)

The organismic, humanist, or *Third Force* (cf. Maslow, 1998: 3; Bell and Taylor, 2004: 445) body of psychological knowledge hence burgeoned as distinct from behaviorist, Freudian and psychoanalytic movements, based on its conception of the human being, overall focus and methodological assumptions. It also emerged as a reaction against Descartes' mind–body dualism, a focus on the negative traits of humanity, and assumptions that the environment is all-powerful in determining human action. Naturally, various humanist theorists could be proposed that do not fit snugly into this somewhat generalizing summation, but Hall and Lindzey suggest that: "organismic theory is more of an attitude or orientation or frame of reference than it is a systematic behavior theory" (1960: 329), enabling its use as a relative point of comparison, having drawn primarily from some of the most prominent and founding actors, to assess its correlation with, and influence on, positive psychology.

Positively humanist?

There indeed seem to be a number of striking similarities between the two schools of thought, confirming the claims of Resnick *et al.* (2001: 74), Mahoney (2005: 745), Gable and Haidt (2005: 104), and Fineman (2006: 273). Both focus on and refer specifically to "positive," "healthy" and "normal" traits rather than the negative or pathological, and assume they are inherent to the human agent. This reduces the agency afforded by each to the environment in shaping human action, thought and motivation. Further, humanistic theory's (re)uniting of the psychological and physiological recalls positive psychology's call for *duality*, when considering the positive and negative as two constitutional, inseparable parts of the holistic human being. Goldstein's theory of harmonizing tension furthers this notion of balance so integral to Seligman *et al.* The notion of *self-actualization* is proffered by Goldstein as the central drive in human life, and refers to the innate strive to realize one's inherent potential (cf. Hall and Lindzey, 1960: 298), very reminiscent of "positive psychology and the positivity movement in general" (Fineman, 2006: 272) and also to an extent the assertion that an individual's happiness and well-being are their desired outcomes (cf. Seligman, 2003: 127). Finally, both Maslow and Seligman have openly proclaimed they wish to *improve life* rather than merely observe it.

There are then clear resonances between the two, and Seligman even accepts that Allport and Maslow are *distinguished ancestors* of his progeny (2005: 7). Bell and Taylor equally assert that Maslow (and Fromm) were "primarily important" as "cultural visionaries or prophetic voices" for the subsequent "human potential movement" (2004: 440). Martin, however, highlights one pronounced distinction that emerges from this analysis: "[Positive psychology's] manifesto could have been written by humanistic psychologists such as ... Abraham Maslow, but positive psychologists aspire to be far more experimentally oriented than them" (Martin, 2007: 89).

Whereas Allport warned against *operationism*, emphasizing the minutiae of measurement and its intentional translation to a pragmatic application in an "action setting" (cf. Hall and Lindzey, 1960: 260), the positive psychology literature is fraught with references to objective measurement, comparisons, classifications, and practical techniques and interventions. A "growing breach" (Taylor, 2001: 14) has thus resultantly occurred between these two psychologies, with Seligman publicly turning his back on, what could arguably be described as, his heritage.

Despite the similarities outlined above, there are three reasons given by Seligman as to why humanistic psychology is "not representative" of positive psychology: namely, "they have generated no research tradition, are narcissistic, and are antiscientific" (cited in Taylor, 2001: 13). Taylor responds in the *Journal of Humanistic Psychology* to each of these charges in turn. The first, he informs, results from an epistemological difference, whereby:

> Whatever could be claimed as research literature, Seligman would likely deny was real scientific research—on the grounds that the N was too small, or the sample was too biased, or there was no control group, or the study was based on mere self-report, and so on.
>
> (ibid.: 17)

This seems a fairly effective riposte, due to the evidently varying fundamental metatheoretical preconditions held by positive and humanistic psychology, in general, for what one could consider methodologically sound, the other may well disregard on principle. The indictment of narcissism too stems from a similar battle of episteme, recalling Allport's distinction between *idiographic* and *nomothetic* approaches. Where Allport, and presumably Taylor, would value individual, subjective analyses, Seligman would likely favor more objective, universal, general principles for investigation and theorizing. To the nomotheticist: "any form of self-absorption is narcissistic ... self-knowledge, intuition, insight, the interpretation of one's dreams ... must remain completely foreign to [those] who demand that all science be a definition of reality defined exclusively by the senses and the intellect" (ibid.: 21–2). So, for the scientist concerned with objectifying the subjective—as Seligman proclaims he is (2003: 127)—despite relying partially on individual testimonies regarding a subject's own happiness, the desire to rationally objectify would conceivably render a contrary, deliberate focus on any one individual a narcissistic act.

To the final allegation of being antiscientific (also reported in Held, 2004: 10), Taylor implies that Seligman has confused humanism, an historically viable movement in academic psychology, with "the psychotherapeutic counterculture ... [found in] your local crystal shop where all manner of incense and astrological influences are purveyed" (2001: 22). Compellingly, Seligman and Csikszentmihalyi somewhat reinforce Taylor's accusation in an article in *American Psychologist* published in 2000, where they initially praise the "generous vision" of the humanistic psychology movement, but then dismiss it, claiming: "unfortunately, [it] did not attract much of a cumulative empirical base, and ... spawned myriad therapeutic self-help movements" (cited in Held, 2004: 26). Disregarding the number of self-help gurus and therapists who either directly or indirectly allude to positive psychology and its central preoccupations, and Seligman's desire to enable individuals to help themselves, the generation of subsequent, discrete popular movements that may share humanistic psychology's desires and world-view does not de facto justify its rejection as an intellectual discipline. In the words of the television presenter Noel Edmonds, who publicly avows his belief in positivity: "You don't have to sit cross-legged, with beads round your neck, eating only lentils, to believe in it" (2006: 26).

Taylor then enquires whether these divergent viewpoints can ever be reconciled (ibid.: 14). Held offers an interesting insight that despite spokespersons for the discipline trying tirelessly to differentiate positivity, "not only from humanistic psychology but from the rest of psychology (and social science) as well" (Held, 2004: 36), they may not actually be that different after all. For, as positive psychologists "claim not to deny *evil facts* of any sort," he asks: "are [they really] that different from *negative psychologists*?", who study "what is wrong with us ... in the positive hope of better living too" (ibid.: 39, emphasis in original). Hence, Martin affords that positive psychology may differ only in degree from its humanistic predecessor (2007: 90), and if so, Seligman may then be rushing to exclude on *a priori* grounds both the very tradition his own theory represents (Taylor, 2001: 13) and the rest of a field from which he is not overly differentiated from.

A mainstream counter-culture

> It is probably true quite generally that in the history of human thinking the most fruitful developments frequently take place at those points where two different lines of thought meet.
>
> (Werner Heisenberg, 2009: 130)

The preceding account has introduced and outlined positive psychology and some of its major actors and the cultural spread of its objects and templates, its historical and mythic origins; and its idealized, promoted subject positions—notably akin to *Homo happicus*. Comments upon its theoretical and philosophical positioning can now then be made with a degree of confidence. The evidence shows that it is an approach certainly individualist and humanist in essence, but based upon rationalist and instrumentalist predicates regarding how to understand and study the human agent: "we are, unblushingly, scientists first" (Seligman, cited in Held, 2004: 27).

This is not an unprecedented observation. Taylor asserts that the senior proponents of positive psychology are "all" products of the discipline of behaviorism, and have "not only committed themselves to the superiority of empirical data, but they have also generally no training in epistemology other than the behavioristic" (2001: 15). He even goes so far as to declare that: "there is no positive psychology except that which is established through reductionist quantitative analysis" (ibid.: 17). This is echoed in his belief that the Templeton Foundation favors only "reductionist psychology" (ibid.: 27), and that, in this context, "positive means positivism" (ibid.: 15).

This then demands the question: *How has positive psychology been able to successfully amalgamate humanistic traditions and concerns with a rejection of traditional humanist methods of enquiry?* It could be substantiated that the discipline has forged itself as a *hybrid*, taking particularly from both humanism and positivism the elements it found most appealing. Importantly, it is recognized within the literature, and even by positive psychologists themselves, that such an event has occurred. Fineman suggests that: "It takes over, claim its proponents, where 'positive thinking' gurus leave off, by applying rigorous scientific method to the folk nostrums of positivity" (2006: 270). Heisenberg's epigraph that opens this section thus seems to ring true, that *fruitful developments* can occur when two conceptually *different lines of thought meet*. As Martin states:

> Positive psychologists might view themselves as making moral judgments which they integrate with current science, whether they are doing psychotherapy, writing self-help books, or pursuing other forms of applied psychology. They might also admit that their emphasis on positive health ... is moral-laden in ways that shape their research ...
>
> On the other hand, positive psychologists might view themselves as empirically oriented in that they are simply doing science ... they are merely reporting scientific discoveries when they speak to the public in self-help books and through therapeutic interventions. They are not making moral judgments—at least not beyond those all scientists make.
>
> (2007: 90)

However, as to whether this hybridization results in a strong, practical and valid science is a matter of debate. Martin, in particular, discusses a number of "red flags" that emerge when positive psychology tries to conduct itself as both a morally-laden *and* morally-neutral science (ibid.: 94). It can be argued then that it either suffers from not fully appreciating the relative incommensurability of its opposing intellectual traditions or, contrastingly, that it is actually strengthened, in terms of its cultural and discursive resonance, by drawing upon and reproducing some of the most prominent, albeit somewhat contradictory, mythic foundations of the modern era.

"It was all like the 1960s—but with a difference" (Heelas, 1992: 155)

It was alluded to by Maslow that every historical age "but ours" had its conceptual ideal: "All of these have been given up by our culture; the saint, the hero, the gentleman, the knight, the mystic" (1998: 17). He proffered though that "we" may soon adopt the subject position of the "self-fulfilling human being"—a principal aspect of positive and humanistic psychology – to fill this void:

> The discourse of "self-development" and "self-actualization" is employed by many therapists, counsellors, healers ... is used in countless books and articles ... [and] enters into the delibera-tions of middle-class people in their thirties and forties living in Islington, or who have dropped out, perhaps to live in the Celtic fringe.
>
> (Heelas, 1992: 141)

Layard demonstrates the accuracy of Heelas' above observation, and Maslow's prediction, by indicating that this image or ideal "could well become the psychological basis of twenty-first-century culture" (2005: 9). Whether or not one is an advocate of positivity and its assumptions, it is ultimately hard to deny the prevalence of and support for their impacts, techniques and promoted morality and subject positions extant throughout academic, political and cultural spheres.

The drive for positivity hence reflects and supports the two previ-ously discussed *shocks* that have resulted in the *circuits of happiness*, as converts/patients/customers are all invited throughout various facets of their lives to shake off Kafkaesque notions of restrictive environ-mental conditions and embark on *the project of your life*, becoming "the philosopher of your own happiness" (Schoch, 2006: viii). The fact that positive psychology is an amalgam of individualist and humanistic interests, and antithetical rationalist and instrumentalist techniques of analysis and understanding thus enables it to relate, at least on some level, to a wider array of potentially sympathetic audiences. Acceptance of a hybridized mythic perspective (cf. Latour, 1993), after a cultural dearth of those more holistic, is not too unusual; Brooks argues that voluminous peculiar juxtapositions (2000: 9) have emerged as a "cultural consequence of the information age" (ibid.: 11). He declares in fact that the grand achievement of the 1990s was to "create a way of living that lets you be an affluent success *and* ... a free spirited rebel" (ibid.: 42, emphasis in original), a similar mantra to that of positive psychology. In addition to the earlier Thriftian discussions of the subject position of the *fast subject*, Boltanksi and Chiapello (2005) articulate that the "profound irony" of the era of modern capitalism is the manner in which the "social and artistic critiques that flowered," in this account in the 1960s, have since "been incorporated into [its] management ideology" (cf. Turner, 2007: 412).

Although not referring to positivity directly, Heelas offers an interesting insight in a discussion of sacralization, the self and contemporary capitalism that can apply here. Despite Seligman's objections to the New Age endeavor (recall Taylor, 2001: 13), it can be argued that a strong aspect of positive psychology's cultural authority actually comes from the taking of a "distinctive portrayal of the self" modeled on an optimistic humanism—embodied by Wright and Lopez's request: "label us hopeful optimists (please)" (2005: 42)—that emerged in the "hippie" counterculture resulting from a reaction against the capitalist mainstream, and combining it with a scientific, pragmatic discourse, rendering a seductive image of how to live as inherently achievable and reproducible for individuals, companies and governments (Heelas, 1992: 139).

The counter-culture model of the self in question was part of the "cultural revolution of the 1960s," and based on authenticity, liberation, self-religion and expressivism, being principally consumed with discovering "one's true nature" by "delving within" (ibid.). Much like Seligman, Maslow and their respective supporters, it foremost assumed that salvation, happiness and success all stem from the internal, "sovereign" arena of human agency (ibid.: 148) and not one's environment. Layard hence reports that many of the ideas in positive psychology "have recurred throughout the ages in all the religious traditions that focus on the inner life ... in every case techniques are offered for liberating the positive in all of us, which religious people call divine" (2005: 9).

Significantly, this model of the self forwarded by beatnik iconoclasts, and seemingly adopted by humanistic and positive psychologies, relies on a *sacralized* image, where that which is external has been marginalized to the extent that even the divine has been internalized: "*We are God*" (Heelas, 1992: 146, emphasis in original). This very much recalls Dawkins' denouncement that the Templeton Foundation favors science that is willing to "say something nice about religion" (2006: 19) and their founder's comments in the Preface of Snyder and Lopez's *Handbook of Positive Psychology* (2005a). The "essential thrust" of the "humanist" and "psychological" concerns are then "identical," wherein "as befits this monastic identification of Self with God … [they] might talk of 'empowerment', vitality and increased creativity" (Heelas, 1992: 146–7).

However, while the counter-culture was generated from a reaction against mainstream capitalism, positive psychology is arguably taking steps to (re)unite this model of how humankind *is* and *can* be with "new" capitalistic (recall Thrift, 2005b), political and organizational conceptualizations of the individual: "That the seminar room has taken over from LSD and other transformational devices should not blind us to the continuities" (Heelas, 1992: 152). Heelas marvels at the "extraordinary" extent to which these two antagonistic viewpoints are being merged: "[W]ork is understood to be a spiritual discipline … participants suppose that they have the opportunity to 'work' on themselves, thereby actualizing the God within" (ibid.: 157).

Politicians, organizations and individuals can then now, by embracing the myths and image of *Homo happicus*, put forward by the mass-discursive, cultural phenomenon of utilitarianist, human relations and positive psychology "forces of identity" (recall Thrift, 1999: 52) become part of an enlightened revolution while working in conjunction with the mainstream economy: there is no need to "drop out" entirely in order to "pursue the quest that lies within" (Heelas, 1992: 161). The ideals of the 1960s have undergone a twenty-first-century revamp, and in no small part due to the actors, objects and templates of the positivity drive.

Seligman's "Manhattan Project for the social sciences" (1999) has thus indeed had a remarkable effect on Anglo-American culture, acutely enabling the core actants and myths of the Happiness Agenda to become embedded in the conceptions and actions of the micro-individual realm. It has contributed to relocating "the turn to the self" from a peripheral, informal, anti-organizational counterculture to the mainstream of contemporary political and corporate theorizing and activity, and even highlighted and enhanced a burgeoning focus on the spiritual, as favored by Sir John Templeton. Smail thus determines that such ideas tend to flourish: "a) because we so want it to be effective, and b) because it's impossible to demonstrate that it isn't effective" (1993: 16), perhaps a telling indictment of the true discursive appeal and power of being *positive*, and its place in the modern political, organizational and individual cultural circuits of the pursuit of happiness.

5
Happy days

> Although I flit over a vast continent of Western
> scholarship, it is only in the capacity of an anthro-
> pological tourist, collecting an intellectual geneal-
> ogy here and a fragment of academic folklore there,
> while making a most superficial inspection of the
> great philosophical monuments.
>
> (Sahlins, 1996: 395)

Concurring with the above words of Sahlins, the review in the
preceding chapters of the history, structure and champions of the
cultural circuits of happiness in the modern Anglo-American era has
swept over a "vast continent" of theoretical and historical "monu-
ments" (ibid.: 395), highlighting Thrift's characteristic conception
that: "all manner of times are constructed by the particular networks that thread their way ... around the world" (1999: 63). In
"The Sacralization of the Self in New Age Capitalism," Heelas asks
the poignant and pertinent question: "Why have so many people
in the West come to believe in them*selves*?" (1992: 147, emphasis
in original). The arguments and evidence in this book pertaining to
happiness are thus able to provide one possible answer.

Notably, this *turn to the self* is understandable most explicitly in
relation to the "major socio-cultural developments" outlined, and
the alignment of their "various trajectories which have been long in
the making" (ibid.). These have been argued as, typically of such phenomena, comprising a patchwork of the political, economic and cultural within society. It is appropriate now then to provide a summary

of that determined so far, below in the first section, and to address, in the next section, one of the emergent facets of the Happiness Agenda not yet explicitly considered: its *spiritualization*.

Knowing happiness

> [These events] can easily be interpreted as a lan-
> guage of the self and self-making—there are emer-
> gent properties, there is self-organization, and so
> on ... [T]hey have provided a new vehicle for dis-
> semination of older and more general New Age and
> New Age-y ideas ... [T]hey have provided symbolic
> authority ... the use of "scientific" metaphors adds
> a touch of legitimacy.
>
> (Thrift, 1999: 49)

The preceding chapters of this book have formulated and utilized a conceptual framework by which to conceive of the "modern" Anglo-American ideological developments regarding happiness as a coherent *agenda*. Establishing how it operates via a "series of relations" (cf. Thrift, 2005b), through and upon objects, actors and templates; demonstrating that the circulation of discursive, cultural networks can be expatiated by formulating a propitious "map of where counts" (Thrift, 1999: 52). It has been asserted that such contingents transpired as a result of interrelated epiphenomena or *shocks* occurring at different historical and sociological junctures; wherein certain foundational *myths* about how Anglo-American society views itself have increased in prominence in the last three hundred or so "Enlightened" years. These myths are: individualism, humanism, rationalism and instrumentalism; and have underpinned the pervasive preoccupation with the deliberate and proactive pursuit of happiness.

The three shocks or "main poles of innovation" (ibid.) alluded to are: the nineteenth-century macro-utilitarian political appropriation of happiness; the twentieth-century meso-assimilation of this politicized interpretation within organizational practice and unitaristic human relations theorizing; and the twenty-first-century micro-realm employment of it in a hedonistic and personally affective positivity, advocated by influential disciplines of social psychology. While chronologically disparate, the striking mythological and practical concomitancy of these events has contributed greatly to the circulation within contemporary Anglo-American society of certain, bespoke definitional and characteristic ideas regarding happiness. Namely, that it is: pursuable and attainable; can be provided through appropriate legislative policy and personal responsibility; may be measured scientifically; is located within the individual; and is actionable in correlation with the surrounding capitalistic structure. This provides a coherent narrative as to how the rhizomatically emergent cultural obsession with being happy is founded upon the related preoccupations of our politics, organizations and individuals; resulting in a prevailing, collaborative strive by embedded willing human agents towards the subject position of *Homo happicus*.

As depicted in Figure 1.1 on p. 44, the similarities and interactions regarding happiness occurring between the three realms substantiate their collective promotion, wherein utilitarian, human relations and positivity vocabularies, using these as respective, identifiable archetypes, have come to validate one another symbiotically forming a tripartite circulatory mechanism. By occurring at and across the macro, meso and micro levels of society, they thus form and sustain an encompassing *extraordinary discursive apparatus* (recall Thrift 2005b: 6), the actants in each and any realm constantly (re)asserting those in the other two. In addition to these "innovate poles," this framework is suffused with the activities of: scientists, economists, philosophers, psychologists, politicians, authors, academics, managers, self-help gurus, media outlets and members of the general public in it, who *generate* and *distribute* mythically commensurable ideas concerning happiness via the respective dissemination of their: political policies, books, debates, conversations, DVDs, scholarly publications and presentations, televised programmes and magazine articles, school curricula, corporate initiatives and seminars.

These *actors* and *objects* that populate the Happiness Agenda hence promote particular ways of "doing" and "being" to their particular *audiences*—be they citizens, employees or individuals. Encouraging them to accept these ways of seeing the world and themselves, in congruence with the surrounding, validating cultural backdrop to which they all contribute. This collusion (not a word used to infer any deliberately orchestrated intent or Machiavellian scheming) creates an "appropriate milieu, a welcoming territory" (recall Goodchild, cited in Thrift, 1999: 31), by providing a system of internal consistency, or, as described in the Introduction, *a social conspiracy of coordination* between modern Anglo-American people and their actions in accordance with socially desirous images; that is only exposed by conducting a "history of the present." By "repeating themselves and one another again and again," common thoughts, myths and practices regarding the peculiar present enactment and definition of happiness have then contemporarily come to successfully "organize human life [and] manifest their own truth in their performance" (ibid.).

Thus, this cultural network of actants combines with the shocks to form a rhizomatic, multi-levelled "river of communication" (recall Thrift, 2005c: 24), composed of: events, beliefs, texts and acts; that collectively produce a very seductive image of *how to be* (happy) in the modern age, wherein a rational focus on one's individualized, hedonistic happiness is presently morally defensible—providing a possible answer to Heelas' question regarding why have so many people "come to believe in themselves"—for those who wish to act in accordance with what have become commonly accepted political, organizational and personal norms.

The happy death of god

> God is dead. God remains dead. And we have killed him. How shall we comfort ourselves, the murderers of all murderers? What was holiest and mightiest of all that the world has yet owned has bled to death under our knives: who will wipe this blood off us? What water is there for us to clean ourselves? What festivals of atonement, what sacred games shall we have to invent? Is not the greatest of this deed too great for us? Must we ourselves not become gods simply to appear worthy of it?
>
> (Nietzsche, 1974: section 125)

In addition to establishing the existence and nature of the cultural circulation of happiness, the relationship between the societal levels at which it occurs, and its manifestation in numerous actors, objects and templates, a prominent facet which cannot be overlooked is how this contemporarily coordinated agenda has seemingly become embraced as a secularized system of faith, whereby in the cultural context of Anglo-Americans increasingly coming to "believe in themselves," explicated above, exponents minister to the willing masses the virtues of self-work, self-belief and self-worship as methods by which to achieve personal happiness.

Accordingly, Bell and Taylor afford that in recent years the traditional conceptualization of religion in Western societies has undergone a "diffusion" in political and social arenas; and especially so in the fields of management and organizational development: "which is dominated by a discourse of intrinsic motivation, commitment, empowerment, personal growth and self-actualization" (2004: 440). This is proposed as being a reflection of increased affluence and material comfort of a set demographic of the population: "predominantly … white, male, mid-life professionals who, having achieved material wealth and security, find themselves looking for alternative sources of meaning" (ibid.). As demonstrated in Chapter 2, preceding hegemonic "medieval world views" wherein one's identity was generally provided in relation to the prevailing social order and "a God envisioned as being 'other' than the human realm" (ibid.: 148) have come to be eroded. As Smail surmises: "We have tried an authoritarian God, and that didn't work. We have tried both the majesty of the King and the dictatorship of the proletariat, and they brought us only grief" (1993: 199).

In light of the opening quote from Nietzsche, it can be sustained that this has occurred, in no small part, as a consequence of the, aforediscussed, rationalist and instrumentalist assault of the Enlightenment on traditional religion in conjunction with the occurrence of the Industrial Revolution. It was also amplified by the "tendency to individualization induced by market pressures, the disintegration of the public sphere, the privatization of morals" and the societal embracement of overtly humanistic undertakings (ibid.: 196–7), whereby the profaning "death" (or marked decrease in prominent, mostly unchallenged mythic discourse) of other-worldly gods and the inevitable "alienating consequences of modern industrial society" (Bell and Taylor, 2004: 444) left a relative emotional and personal void in the moral, political and organizational structuring of Anglo-American society. As inferred by Maslow (1998: 1), see Chapter 4, it was into this gap which the post-materialist and self-expressive New Age "counter-cultures," notably including *the pursuit of happiness,* could come to be reified and rendered as sacred and holy, and widely embraced as a much-needed replacement.

Such an occurrence presumes that human beings inherently need something to "wrap their lives around," and with the increasing dearth of external benevolent or wrathful gods, many, it seems, have looked to notions of individualized and internalized spirituality, wellness and happiness:

> The shattering of that part of our personhood which is structured by "form" is experienced as the kind of pain which cries out to be assuaged by the comfort of association. As the last resort people seem to seek refuge and stability by huddling together on any moral high ground.
>
> (Smail, 1993: 200)

Concurring with this line of argument, Calás and Smircich report that numerous company leaders and agents within the media have been overtly interested in "spirituality and business" since the early 1990s, and that this has spread noticeably into "the areas of business, management, and organizations, as well as [becoming] a focus for academic conferences and management consultant practices" (2003: 327). Long and McLeod even suggest that: "it is currently the most published new topic in business school literature"; and provide a review of the work of numerous scholars disseminating throughout the field (2006: 56).

They offer a classificatory system by which a majority of that written can be categorized into one of what they consider to be four general themes, being: "(1) its contribution to organizational performance; (2) the spiritual development of the manager as an agent of organization; (3) individual level spirituality; [and] (4) whether scientific methods can be used to research [it]" (ibid.). Interestingly, and in conformance with the noted increasing scarcity of traditional faith in external god-figures, their functioning definition of *workplace-*spirituality welcomes any discussion that considers it as behavior "guided by values and principles" or "as a state of transpersonal or intrapersonal transcendence," but does not cater for "spirituality as religious commitment" (ibid.: 56–7). By far the most prolific theme in the literature they reviewed was the first, attempts to discuss or promote the positive relationship between nurturing employee spirituality and achieving organizational objectives. This has striking parallels with the human relations-inspired assumptive link between happiness and productivity discussed at length in Chapter 3. One of the papers they reviewed even instrumentally states as though it were an irrefutable fact: "[A company whose] work environment responsively supports ... and fosters spiritual development, *will* realise heightened individual and organizational performance" (ibid.: 58, emphasis added).

It is of significance that within the four generic themes identified by the authors, very few writers were primarily concerned with discussing spirituality, in the workplace or otherwise, as emanating from or being reinforced by a wider cultural movement. Calás and Smircich do, however, suggest that the spiritual proliferation attested to has occurred widespread as a "response to contradictions" inherent in the modern world "faced by so many" (2003: 327). They then question whether this is a "stance consistent with privatization and globalization? Part of an ethical renewal the world over? [Or] linked to other more fundamental social changes?" (ibid.). They ultimately conclude, though, alternatively, that the increase in spirituality is actually none of these and is moreover: "a means to counteract self-interest at a time when all other messages seem to point in the opposite direction" (ibid.). However, it is possible to disagree with such a contention; as when conceived of in terms of the nature and spread of the Happiness Agenda, the increased embrace of spirituality is indeed understandable in relation to the cumulative mythic social shifts, or *shocks*, that have manifested in an ethical and social "renewal" throughout Anglo-American society. Furthermore, the spiritual elements of the pervasive conception of happiness are arguably very much an advocacy of self-interest, rather than a lone stanchion attempting to stem the tide of individualism.

Bell and Taylor surmise then that the array of seminars and workshops promoting self-fulfilment in relation to work, dubbed "Spiritual Management Development" (SMD), in organizations are indeed an endeavor to encourage employees' engagement "with an inner self"; and, equally, that it is "social movements" that have enabled such "diffusion of religious practices into secular life" (2004: 439). They further report that such activity has become conspicuous in a variety of practices: "To this end, a vast array of techniques are employed, including meditation, guided visualization, self-hypnosis, neuro-linguistic programming, therapeutic touch, bio-feedback, yoga, walking on fire, and inducing altered states of consciousness" (ibid.: 442). The authors thus infer that fundamental to SMD, and again already postulated herein as of equal importance to the Happiness Agenda, are the notions of: individualism; the self being central to both "personal and corporate salvation"; and direct, active and embedded engagement *with*, rather than *without*, the capitalist system (ibid.). Recalling once more the discussions in Chapter 4 of an expressive, self-focused "counter-culture" being assimilated by the circuits of "new" capitalism (cf. Boltanksi and Chiapello, 2005), and striking an accord with Heelas' iconic description of a burgeoning "religion for yuppies" heralded by "angels in pinstripes" (1992: 140).

A religiosity of the Self

Having attended to some of the theoretical similarities between the *spiritual* and *happiness* movements, it can then be contended that the Happiness Agenda indeed has many requisite components of more traditional belief systems. These include: a connection to an alternate *higher realm*, being the uncapped potential of human performance, and the possibility of *transcendence* to that place, encapsulated by Maslovian prophecies of the passage to a state of "self-actualization." This can occur provided faith is not lost, as people who cannot attain or perform at such levels are often considered not to have employed the requisite techniques sufficiently, and can thus be excommunicated or disregarded. There are also representations of an antithetical realm, described for example in Christian mythology as "Hell," for those trapped in the negative cycle of "learned helplessness" (Seligman, 1975).

Furthermore, the Agenda can boast spiritual *leaders* and *gurus*: influential and charismatic figureheads such as Bentham, Mayo, Maslow and Seligman; *believers* and *missionaries*, their intellectual "converts" who act as disciples in supporting and extolling their philosophies; and clear sets of *rules*: such as those forwarded by the proponents of positive psychology and utilitarianism in their provision of systematic calculations regarding what happiness is and how it can be measured and provided. There is also the requirement for *confessions*, in the form of the abounding questionnaires available intended to ascertain one's level of happiness; which themselves require *inner reflection*, similar to the act of prayer, where quiet, composed meditative states focusing on that which is buried within are often advocated. There are even *articles of communication*: the copious publications available, transmitted through journals, newspapers, the Internet, and television shows; and *sites of worship*, such as in school classrooms and the workplace SMD activities discussed above by Bell and Taylor (2004: 439). Finally and most importantly, there is a *god*—albeit one who is not resident in an other, non-human realm, but is essentially thyself: worshipped through self-focus, self-work, and self-fulfilment, deifying the individual to a position of unassailable prominence:

> Self religions [have recently] expanded and proliferated ... Ultimate celebration is offered. Participants can scarcely be elevated any further. God has, so to speak, come down to earth. Heaven lies in the here and now, to be experienced in this life rather than after death.
>
> (Heelas, 1992: 139)

While the vocabularies utilized within the Happiness Agenda are certainly more "psychological" than explicitly spiritual: "the highly optimistic beliefs concerning innermost human nature smack of a Pelagian-like leap of faith" (ibid.: 143), contemporary moral, social and even spiritual obligations are hence not to an external higher being or even to others, but primarily to oneself (again answering Heelas' earlier cited question); in accordance with the utilitarian idiom of securing "the greatest happiness for the greatest number" via increases effected at the level of the individual. As: "that which lies within is explicitly sacralized ... this is the essence of enlightenment" (ibid.: 146). Consequently, the influence of this spiritualization of happiness is so remarkable that:

> No story has ever spoken so much or shown so much. Not even the ministers of the gods ever made them talk in such a continuous, detailed, and imperative way as the producers of revelations and rules do these days in the name of current reality.
>
> (de Certeau, 1988: 185)

Many agents pursuing happiness have then presently embraced an: "internalized, detraditionalized religiosity, where autonomy and freedom are highly valued and authority lies with the exercise of self-responsibility" (Bell and Taylor, 2004: 443). This has occurred to such a palpable extent that this spiritual translation is itself perhaps even akin to a fourth ideological *shock* in the Happiness Agenda, that supplements the previous three discussed. The outlined spiritualistic undertones of the endeavor to be happy, sustained by its prominence and naturalization within society and that has the compositional and mythological structure of a religious movement; contributes to the prominence of proudly individualistic and self-focusing subject positions, and the cultural circulation of utilitarian, human relations and positive "forces of identity" (recall Thrift, 1999: 52). It seems most apt then that, in the wake of Anglo-American modernity, Enlightened, Industrialized, "rational man" has so effectively killed God, and replaced him with the (aspiring to be) happy Self.

6
Happiness needs practice

> Much is on offer, people are being provided the
> opportunity to meditate, use crystals . . . take
> celebratory-cum-inspirational holidays, participate
> in workshops, become involved with covens, camps
> communes, austere spiritual paths, well organized
> new and not-so-new religious movements or simply
> obtain the cultural provisions (literature, music,
> crafts) which have proliferated in recent times.
> (Heelas, 1996: 140)

Having established the relevance of the spiritualistic embodiment of
happiness in modern Anglo-American society, attention must now turn
to the final prominent issue relating to its cultural dissemination and
embracement. Bell and Taylor, once more, offer an interesting insight
in their comment that although it is relatively commonplace "to note
the progressive diffusion of religious and New Age philosophies into
secular contexts, especially in business and management ... rarely
have researchers explored the *processes* and *practices* entailed in this
diffusion" (2004: 451, emphasis added). While many of these have
indeed been considered in the preceding discussions of the existence
of and relations between objects, subjects, templates and subject positions, most, however, also account for *how* agents attempt to utilize
or even subvert the pull of the Happiness Agenda and its actants to
comport themselves in culturally reinforced ways.

The arguments presented above pertaining to the sociological
realms demonstrate that, first, the Agenda *is* existent but, of equal

importance, second, it is *not* all-consuming and all-producing: people in modern Anglo-American society do not all pursue happiness in the same way. There are countless ways in which audiences interact with the macro-, meso- and micro-realm objects and templates as they see fit, translating them to best suit the complex, contextual and essentially human environment they are to be employed within. Its utilization is thus inescapably expressive of human agency and how it tendentiously finds a space for itself *within* the pervasive cultural agendas at play.

Researcher and practitioner focus, however, can often prioritize the polarized rejection or adoption of (or relative power of and resistance to) the mythic, theoretical or practical elements of mass-discursive, cultural phenomena, and less on ascertaining why such dynamics are so popular and considered of value. For, as to be expanded upon anon, even to criticize, insult, attack, alter, or attempt to subvert any element of the Happiness Agenda is not only considered "aberrant behavior" (recall Duncan, 2007: 86) but, ironically, acts to "breathe new life back into the reflexive complexity" (Thrift, 2005b; cf. Singleton and Michael, 1993: 234). As discursive formations garner their social existence just as much from malefactors as benefactors, to discuss it in any way (including in this book) is to reify and re-establish its presence.

Efforts that could be described as being deliberate acts of resistance or rejection against the concerted, collective pursuit of happiness, can then counter-intuitively be otherwise understood as actually still being essentially conditioned by and ultimately supportive of the Agenda. To explore this concept in line with the preceding theoretical infrastructure, the following will draw upon both a novel augmentation to classic actor-network theory and another recent emerging interest in social science that can be seen to have gravitated towards "new and exciting interdisciplinary syntheses" (Pea and Brown, 1993: vii), questioning the roles of context, appropriation and practice in human activity (Chaiklin and Lave, 1993).

The appeal of practice

Since the 1990s, novel attempts to think about human life and sociality have pondered on the perceived sovereignty of studying systems, discourses and the individual social agent (Schatzki, 2001). Chaiklin and Lave pose that various mainstream metatheoretical approaches can actually act to hinder the study, interpretation and adequate understanding of human activity (1993: 4) as, concurs Armstrong, they can "systematically allow space for the misrepresentation of reality" (2001: 155). Alternatively, *practice*-based approaches, speaking generically, focus their efforts not simply on the human agent, what it is they may be expressing their agency upon or what forces may have encouraged them to do so, but also on the actual manner in which that expression occurs.

While *the cultural circuits of happiness* argument is not presumed to fully account for all the features of the Agenda, it does inherently and unavoidably retain a "top-down" discourse- and mechanism-based, metatheoretical approach. Practice approaches are alternatively (obviously) involved more directly in the study of *practices*, which are defined as: "arrays of human activity" (Schatzki, 2001: 1), or the: "visible routines and observable (actions) of key individuals" (Blackler and Regan, 2005: 1). Considering practice as: "the inarticulate but ever-present background that is vital for us to negotiate the world around us and make sense of our lives" (Chia, 2004: 32), these theorists take actual practices as their subject matter, and analyse them in relation to and as manifestations of a broader "framework of practice" (Blackler, 2004b: 1). "Knowledge, meaning, human activity, science, power, language, social institutions, historical transformations" and research thus all occur within and are components of the *field of practices*, which is the "total nexus" of human activity (Schatzki, 2001: 2). Persons acting and the social world around them cannot be separated (Chaiklin and Lave, 1993: 4–5), as practices act to "simultaneously underlie" both subjects and objects (Schatzki, 2001: 1).

Similarly to that already argued, practice theories typically assert that relationships between people in "new" capitalist society are developed around *objects*, which Knorr-Cetina refers to as "postsocial relations," "objectual solidarity" and "objectualization" (cited in Blackler, 2004a: v, 3). "Objects" are categorized in terms of a "lack of completeness of being," quite contrary to "our everyday conception" (Knorr-Cetina, 2001: 181). Rather than necessarily having the character of a "closed box," objects can contrastingly be seen as comprising "the capacity to unfold indefinitely" (ibid.). This is used to argue that objects can "never be fully attained" (ibid.). Examples of such "objects," echoing the actor-network and rhizomatic discussions previously, can then include: "the natural environment (as the basis for ecology movements), skydiving (as the foundation of a particular kind of leisure group) and consumer goods (through which consumers categorize themselves)" (Blackler, 2004a: 3). Hence, objects in practice theory do not necessarily need to be solid, tangent and clearly outlined physical entities. They can be: ideas, physical articles, myths, or social structures; or anything that can and already has been conceived of herein as an *actant*.

Further, practices are recognized as most commonly being enacted within institutional frameworks such as forms of organization (Blackler, 2004b: 1), rather than being governed specifically by ideas or theories, resulting in individual behavior being considered as *supra*individual: "it would be a mistake to assume that human agency should be reduced to individual people" (Schatzki, 2002: 2). An example of a practice that can be used to explicate these points in context is *vegetarianism*. To be a vegetarian does not require the employment of "scientific experts or modern laboratory techniques to separate the animal and the vegetable" (Barnes, 2001: 18). Neither does one vegetarian community necessarily follow the exact same dietary prohibitions of another (ibid.). It is not possible to provide a mathematical formulae or algorithm for vegetarianism, as it is not a matter of behaving in ways that can be exhaustively calculated or expressed. Nonetheless: 'Vegetarianism is routinely recognizable as a coherent social activity, we encounter it as custom and practice, and acknowledge that membership of a specific vegetarian community will involve acceptance of its distinctive customs and shared practices' (ibid).

To engage in a practice, then, it is argued, is to participate in something done by a group: those partaken in are learnt from and influenced by other people (ibid.). However, this is not to say that an individual in an isolated geographic location cannot be, for example, a vegetarian or a collaborative participant in the communal pursuit of happiness. Constitutive members and material and theoretical reinforcements of the social collective to which an individual belongs, and from which their practices originate and relate, do not need to be present in terms of any immediate vicinity as they are, as already argued in terms of the Happiness Agenda, imbedded within the wider, surrounding historical, cultural and even spiritual "nexus."

From the complementary perspectives of the circuits model and practice approach, it is then somewhat difficult, if not rather unnecessary, to extricate an individual actor from both the web (or network) of practice in which they are operating and other actants engaged in similar endeavors. A practice, be it completing a happiness questionnaire, displaying either a willing or hostile receptivity to a positivity or spirituality seminar, attempting to alter one's physical and emotional well-being; arguing in a political debate over the virtues of a Happiness Policy; or imploring or disavowing the need for a corporate wellness director: are all emergent results of communal, inter-related and inter-forming actions, thoughts and beliefs, throughout a community or population. The presence and occurrence of each particular practice act to validate and reinforce by acknowledgement the others that are related to it, again as postulated in the circuits argument, increasing the established societal resonance of the entire mass-discursive, cultural phenomenon in question. Even if some or many practices are essentially different or even contradictory to one another in terms of their bespoke deployment, the fact that they still contribute to a greater, common web of practice is the issue of significance.

One particular theorist whose works seem relevant to the analysis of happiness and how it is being conceived of, embraced and acted upon in modernity is Michel de Certeau. His book, *The Practice of Everyday Life* (1988), is a coherent treatise upon the "uses to which modes of social behavior are put" by human agents. Dedicated to *the ordinary man*, it establishes a manner of examining the human agent without denying or reducing consideration to either the "social atomism of individuality" or abstracted meta-theory (ibid.: xi). He stresses that his work is not an undertaking to discuss directly the classic antagonism between individual agency and societal structures, but rather an attempt to render such discussion "possible," by finding a way in which to articulate everyday practices or "ways of operating" as not merely an "obscure background to social activity" but as amenable itself to an orchestrated body of "theoretical questions, methods, categories, and perspectives" (ibid.). He does not, however, allow for *statistical* representations: "[They] can tell us virtually nothing about the currents in this sea theoretically governed by the institutional frameworks," as the processes of "classifying, calculating and tabulating" can "grasp only the material used by

consumer practices … and not the formality proper to these practices, their surreptitious and guileful 'movement', that is, the very
activity of 'making do'" (ibid.: 34–5). The nature of the adoption and
enactment of practices is so diverse that to portray them numerically
or through equations is to reduce or distort what is occurring or even
to miss the point entirely.

De Certeau thus offers a vocabulary with which to articulate how
subjects internalize, reproduce and reformat the concerns of their
contemporaneous modernity—whether positively or negatively—at
the level of collective agency, as his approach calls for "a continuing
investigation into the ways in which users – commonly assumed to be
passive and guided by established rules – operate" (ibid.: xi). It is then
in conjunction with the Foucauldian view that the discursive circulation of the Happiness Agenda, and the innate power and appeal of
the prominent subject positions it generates, allow for the potential-
ity of individuals to embrace *and* resist elements of it as they see fit.

A Misery Agenda?

For de Certeau, the human being exists "before texts" and is inextricably part of the "mass of the audience" (ibid.), privileged by anonymity.
S/he is resultantly impacted upon by discursive enterprises but not
entirely produced by them, being the locus for an "incoherent and
often contradictory plurality" of influences: part of "the number," one
of many, who form a multitude of "language and rationalities that
belong to no one" (ibid.: v, xi). The isolated individual, *per se*, plays
then "no part" in de Certeau's study (ibid.: xi). As indicated above, he
is far more interested in the conglomerate or web of operation—acting,
doing, being—that is engaged in within society at a collective and everyday interactional level. However, he defines his own approach by
demarcating it from Foucault's writings on governmentality, by inti-
mating that *Discipline and Punish* (1991) in particular focuses on the
functional *mechanisms* ("miniscule technical procedures") of power
rather than the institutional *apparatus* it is embedded within (de
Certeau, 1988: xiv). De Certeau warns how this otherwise privileges
attention towards the productive processes rather than the collective
actions of those caught within them. He hence posits:

> If it is true that the grid of "discipline" is everywhere becoming
> clearer and more extensive, it is all the more urgent to discover

how an entire society resists being reduced to it, what popular procedures (also miniscule and quotidian) manipulate the mechanisms of discipline and conform to them only in order to evade them, and finally, what "ways of operating" form the counterpart, on the consumer's (or dominee's?) side, of the mute processes that organize the establishment of socioeconomic order.

(ibid.: xiv)

Following de Certeau, there is then an imperative to understand that as the Happiness Agenda (the "grid of discipline") is proposed as being eminently pervasive yet not all-controlling, just how and why *resistance* to it—(re-)conceived in light of de Certeau as society's collective ability to avoid being "reduced" to a de-individualized and uniform array of activities—occurs in such varied and sometimes quite contradictory "ways of operating," and also why *not* engaging with it in any way is, arguably, seemingly so rare.

The realms of popular culture and the mass media offer a number of artefacts that could certainly be considered a resistive backlash to the societal pressure and urge to be happy, or even as counterpoised efforts to embrace misery. O'Neill declared that in recent years: "a new breed of commentator stormed the worlds of publishing and TV punditry: the grumpy old man (or woman) who believes ... Modern Life is Rubbish" (2005). A recent flurry of books and television "talking-head" programmes can be found as testimony to such a belief, including: the BBC series *Grumpy Old Men* (aired 2003–2006) and *Grumpy Old Women* (aired 2005–2008) and their companion almanacs; the imitative *Grumpy Young Men* (aired 2009) for the Paramount Comedy television station; the Channel 4 production *Best and Worst Places to Live* (aired 2005–2007); the popular sardonic *Idler* website (www.idler.co.uk) and its affiliated books lambasting Britain's *Crap Towns* (Jordison and Kieran, 2003, 2004), *Crap Jobs* (Kieran, 2004) and *Crap Holidays* (Kieran, 2005); the similarly cantankerous *Is It Just Me Or Is Everything Just Shit?: The Encyclopaedia of Modern Life* (McArthur and Lowe, 2006), again with its own supporting website (www.iseverythingshit.co.uk); and the disgruntled miserabilist Charlie Brooker's acerbic programmes *Screenwipe* (2006–2008) and *Newswipe* (2009), his review column "Screenburn" for *The Guardian* newspaper and equally choleric books including *TV Go Home* (2001) and *Dawn of the Dumb: Dispatches from the Idiotic Frontline* (2007).

All of the above examples could indeed be used to substantiate claims of the rise of resistance to the Happiness Agenda and the subject position of *Homo happicus*. However, despite, for example, the tome *Crap Jobs* (Kieran, 2004) being tag-lined as: "[telling] of stress, misery and rebellion in the darkest most satanic warehouses, offices [and] call centres ... in the UK," the cause, purpose and shaping of these acts can be argued as deriving from processes other than how resistance is classically conceived. There are clear differences that need to be expressed between what is occurring here in relation to the Happiness Agenda and more common accounts from the field of industrial and organizational sociology.

To clarify, Ackroyd and Collinson express that, in the second half of the twentieth century, organizations widely came to be viewed as: "sites of dissenting behavior and of resistance to authority" (2004: 305). They analyse a continuum of antagonistic workplace practices, ranging from *resistance*: with connotations of behavior that is overt, principled, and perhaps formally organized; through *misbehavior*: defined as self-conscious rule-breaking; to *dissent*: which foregrounds linguistic or normative disagreement (ibid.: 306). Further, they highlight the potential for other such acts, including: insurrections, riots, strikes, sabotage, absenteeism and mockery. Thompson and Ackroyd likewise surmise that: "industrial sociology at its best has been able to uncover the variety of workplace resistance and misbehavior that lies beneath the surface of the formal and consensual" (1995: 615).

A slight development of this perspective comes from Fleming and Sewell, who suggest that in the "new" capitalist age of "electronic surveillance," "team normalization" and "cultural cleansing," dissent also occurs in far "less obvious places" and ways than those listed above (2002: 857). They offer their concept of "švejkism" drawn from a literary character who resists the discipline of the Austro-Hungarian Imperial Army through "subtle forms of subversion that are invariably "invisible" to his superiors" (ibid.: 859), concluding that the performance of "covert and seditious" acts also occur in the "silent spaces of everyday life" (ibid.: 860).

As is quite evident, the motif of the *recalcitrant worker* is perceived by these authors as being most prominent within Anglo-American organizations and industrial sociology. Despite their relative variations, these exemplar views all conform to a traditional, pluralistic conception of resistance which casts it as a series of actions and mind frames emerging from an antagonistic relationship between opposing parties, with the misbehaving saboteur making deliberate and conscious efforts to undermine, disrupt and even derail the agendas of those in positions of relative authority. However, the practice-informed conceptualization of resistance alluded to in relation to the Happiness Agenda is essentially and ostensibly different in nature and intent. An intriguing argument by Singleton and Michael (1993), returning to the prior discussions of actor-networks and the process of enrolment, will now be used to expose and explore this important distinction.

Ambivalence

Singleton and Michael proffer that central to customary narratives about actor-networks is an antipathetic focus on actants' "dramatic triumphs and betrayals" (1993: 229): the flourishing or failure of a particular series of connected actors in achieving their own or imposed ends depends on the successful, firm and lasting "enrolment" of purpose and identity to individual entities. They suggest, however, that this perspective is actually quite misleading, as the act is "not a unilateral process of imposition" but otherwise rather an "arrangement of assent" (ibid.: 229), as power is not exclusively and inescapably delegated by certain actors unto others, but a reciprocal and interactional process in which all the members of a network impact, to varying degrees, on one another. They thus afford the "metaphor" of actors' *ambivalence*, "towards their own and others' attributed network roles," to provide alternative and useful insight (ibid.: 227).

This is very much an interdisciplinary concept, occurring across sociology, urban and ethnicity studies, and geography (cf. Diken, 1998), and is used to refer to the 'processes of identification and distancing" inherent to actants' interactions with one another and their networks (Kosmala, 2006). From this approach, delegated positions or roles within networks are not deemed as altogether fixed or finite, and Singleton and Michael contend that a network is actually rendered durable by the very fact that its constituent elements have the fluidity to occupy its "margins" and the "core" in terms of how much proactive support they offer: "the most outspoken critics and the most ardent stalwarts are simultaneously insiders and outsiders" (1993: 232; cf. Kosmala, 2006). While such mutability for actors to both strengthen *and* snag their encompassing network may seem to threaten its overall integrity, the authors offer engaging empirical evidence to demonstrate that it can actually enforce it; by tracing "ambivalence"—definable then as an actant's capacity for dual-status as insider and outsider—as at once subverting and sustaining the network of the UK Cervical Screening Programme (CSP) (Singleton and Michael, 1993: 234).

The current process of screening for cervical cancer under the British National Health Service (NHS) rests, as in any network, on a series of alliances and associations between a variety of actants: the Government, General Practitioners (GPs), medical researchers and technicians, health promotion officers, feminist commentators, lay women and cervical cells (ibid.: 228). At the time of their publication, this complex medical and social procedure was supposedly "de-problematized" by deliberately "black-boxing," or enrolling, all the elements of the CSP, including its key diagnostic tool the Cervical Smear Test, into individual, clearly demarcated roles. Primary research focus on the GPs, however, exposed them as embodying a conduit or "obligatory point of passage" between numerous other actors, and both disseminating information from the laboratories to and gathering it from patients.

The GPs are thus simultaneously describable as being very much *within* the CSP network: accepting the primacy of science, the NHS, smears, and enrolling women into the testing process, but also *outwith* it: being outspokenly cognizant of the possible relative indeterminacy of the results and posing themselves as an "essential fail-safe mechanism" should they consider any results unclear, inappropriate or inaccurate: "an association that binds the GPs into the network can ... tug [them] out" (ibid.: 242). The conscious acts by the NHS to black-box, simplify and generate unitary identities for all actants, akin to a focus on "triumphs and betrayals" in their delegated roles, hence was not deemed responsible for the maintenance of the network: "To overstress uncertainty and multiplicity would be to endanger the governmental CSP and undermine the GP role; yet, to follow unflinchingly the government's model of the GP role would be to render that role unworkable" (ibid.: 259).

It was alternatively the propensity for "ambivalence" to the established authority and validity of the network and the maintenance of multiple identities on the part of the GPs, leading them to becoming called "benevolent adversaries," which is argued to have ultimately strengthened, reproduced and sustained the entire process of screening and treatment (ibid.).

This clearly resonates with the previously stated "to-and-fro" fluid circulation of the Happiness Agenda and "performative" ability of its actants to embrace an array of differing and even seemingly contradictory positions within it, without stalling the entire phenomenon. Further, it corresponds directly with and corroborates the above assertion that the expressions of both benefactors and malefactors contribute to its overarching sustainment, as virtually any discourse, whether positive or negative, regarding the notion of being happy in the modern day reproduces, reinterprets and re-presents the modern cultural fascination with it.

Significantly, the array of identified potential actors and objects of "resistance" to the Happiness Agenda listed above, in the guise of misery-enthused pundits, books and television programs, do not occur in the same context as those by downtrodden employees striking back against employers (or even citizens against a state) as studied diligently by Ackroyd and Collinson (2004) *et al*. As opposed to "formally organized, self-conscious" feats of "rule-breaking" (ibid.), the popularized examples of the bemoaning of the stresses and strains of modern life, despite appearances, are defensibly not necessarily indicative of a swelling reaction against the notion of happiness itself or the widespread societal fixation on it—an emerging, countervailing *Misery Agenda*—but, as similarly seen by Singleton and Michael with the GPs, rather conceivable as episodic and symptomatic expressions of discontent at some of the contemporary avenues offered unto employees and citizens through which to achieve it.

They were not treaties imploring a focus on other culturally-sanctioned pursuits and becoming and remaining *un*happy were far from being the ultimate goals of any of these outcries. They are then examples of *ambivalence*, as defined above, towards some of the techniques with which the "crusade" (Furedi, 2006b: 1) to be happy is widely being fought, rather than the endeavor itself. "Grumpy Old Men" and their supporters are arguably so due to a common underlying desire to actually become happy (for if one does not yearn to be happy complaining about not being so has no basis), and are indeed therefore engaging in acts of "resistance" to the Happiness Agenda very much through mechanisms which are influenced by, integral to and, ironically, reproductive of it. To recall Singleton and Michael's terminology, these actors and their actions are simultaneously "outsiders" on the periphery of the network through the expression of their criticisms, and thereby also unavoidably "insiders" residing in its core due to the fact that they are still directly engaging with the concept of happiness: the archetypal "benevolent adversaries" (1993: 259).

This demonstrates that the concept of resistance, particularly in how it is traditionally and commonly conceived, is hence quite problematic, and also why examples of not engaging with happiness in any way whatsoever in the current cultural climate are relatively scarce. Perhaps the only way to not be affected by or contribute, even through dissent, to the Happiness Agenda—and thereby oddly the only way to effectively resist it—is to be entirely unaware of and isolated from any calls to minister to one's own contemporarily individualized, humanized, rationalized and instrumentalized sense of happiness. This would be achievable by residing in a different geo-temporal epoch, or remaining unaffected whatsoever by the politically, organizationally and personally manifest obsessions of the modern Anglo-American age, but such an existence is currently rendered somewhat difficult as such concerns are so central to its present construction.

While individuals may then vehemently disagree with the widely accepted and utilized definition of and striving towards happiness, to express outwardly, or even contemplate internally, such concerns is, again, to still contribute to the overall reproduction of the societal infatuation with it. Following such logic, in terms of the Agenda, it is then arguably of greater scholarly benefit to alternatively conceive of resistance to it as, and focus on, the infinitely varying degrees of culturally influenced "ambivalence" and human appropriation within it, recalling de Certeau's earlier utilized definition of such practices being society's ability to avoid collective "reduction" to a homogeneous display of responses.

Strategies and tactics

Returning to de Certeau, he very much focuses on how "users" (a term he employs quite deliberately and alternatively to *subjects*) "reappropriate the space organized by techniques of sociocultural production," the examination of which reveals the "clandestine forms taken by the dispersed, tactical and makeshift creativity of groups or individuals already caught in the nets" (1988: xiv). It is then more so the network of *anti-discipline* in society, to use Foucault again as a yardstick, which is of interest to him and indeed this final analysis. Phrases such as *making do, tactics* and *uses*, very much correlating with the concept of *ambivalence*, are all found in his exploration of how human agents navigate and actively "consume" the corporately, politically and socially produced subject positions they come into contact with— rather than merely "resist" or "conform" to them.

He posits, as example, that once the images being broadcast via television and the amount of time spent in front of them by certain individuals have been considered, an endeavor numerous studies have been dedicated to, what often still remains unasked is: "what the consumer *makes* of these images and during these hours? ... what do they make of what they 'absorb', receive and pay for? What do they do with it?" (ibid.: 31). It is this that leads de Certeau to refer to human agents as "consumers," or "users"; actors that are inescapably and undeniably capable of, to draw once again a related term from an ANT lexicon, enacting their agency and *translating*, interpreting and "re-using" (ibid.: 30) that which is around them.

He provides as a further example a description of an immigrant living in an alien, society, and the ways in which they *make do* in order to actively survive:

> Thus a North African living in Paris or Roubaix (France) insinu-ates *into* the system imposed on him by the construction of a low-income housing development or of the French language the ways of "dwelling" (in a house of language) peculiar to his native Kabylia. He super-imposes them and, by that combination, cre-ates for himself a space in which he can find *ways of using* the constraining order of the place or of the language ...
>   Without leaving the place where he has no choice but to live and which lays down its law for him, he establishes within it a degree of *plurality* and creativity. By an art of being in between, he draws unexpected results from his situation.
>
> (ibid., emphasis in original)

De Certeau therefore acts as an appropriate segue between the metatheoretical circuits analysis of the Happiness Agenda, how it plays out, spreads and strengthens between its multi-realm sites, and how it impacts upon and is actually used by individuals, be they "ambivalent" or otherwise, on a mundane, regular and personal level—drawing very much upon the "boring as well as the sexy" (recall Thrift, 2005b: 3).

The fundamental "mistake" of certain "systematic thinking about social and cultural issues" is then, concurs Smail: "to underestimate the resourcefulness and adaptability of power, which is as resourceful and adaptable as human ingenuity can make it" (1993: 198). The focus of research should hence not be exclusively towards the "consumer" or the "products" s/he uses, the "indexes of the 'order' which is imposed on him" (de Certeau, 1988: 32) but should also embrace a cognisance of the "gap of varying proportions opened by the use that [is made] of them" (ibid.). It is thus the manner of appropriative interpretation, the way in which changes are effected, "ambivalence" is managed, alterations are devised and utilized, context is created by the agent and their conscious engagement with facets of, say, the Happiness Agenda that is of great interest and importance. As summarized by de Certeau, scholars should ultimately be concerned with the power "battles or games between the strong and the weak, and with the 'actions' which remain possible for the latter" (ibid.: 34).

The way in which de Certeau theorizes upon these power games is by distinguishing within the nexus of human practice between what he terms "strategies" and "tactics." He conceives of a *strategy* as a powerful and pervading "coordination or manipulation of relationships" that is rendered possible by a subject, or group of subjects, be they "a business, an army, a city, [or] a scientific institution," becoming identifiable and as having a common ideological and or functional purpose (ibid.: 35–6). It or they must have a place, or many places, which can (to an extent) be "delimited" and "serve as a base" from which relations with an *exteriority* composed of "targets or threats" can be managed (ibid.). This "place" can be a building, network of structures or even a philosophical and political platform from which to produce discourses, and interact with a network of "objects," as is conceived of equally through the previously presented Thriftian, ANT and practice lexicons. A strategy is then an organized, concerted campaign to bring about particular ends in certain ways, based on rationally structured financial, philosophical and or cultural foundations; the influential power of which is "bounded by its very visibility" (ibid.: 37).

Tactics, by contrast, are: "calculated action[s] determined by the absence of a proper locus" (ibid.: 36–7). They cannot be delimited from an exteriority, because it is essentially that which is external, peripheral and outside to a mainstream strategy. Tactics are "manoeuvres" that operate "on and with a terrain imposed on it and organized by the law of a foreign power," playing out "within the enemy's field of vision ... [and] territory" (ibid.). They are the responses of those who do not have the capacity or resources to plan or execute general, widespread strategies, operating "in isolated actions, blow by blow" as they do not emanate from an established "base" where those employing them "could stockpile its winnings, build up its own position and plan raids" (ibid.). Tactics are the actions of "poachers" operating in the cracks of systemic regimes: "In short, a tactic is an art of the weak" (ibid.: 37), which is effected: "within the order established by the strong" (ibid.: 40). A tactic is determined by the relative "*absence of power* just as a strategy is organized by its postulation" (ibid.: 38, emphasis in original).

This essentially bellicose imagery is very reminiscent of guerrilla-style or "insurgency" warfare, from which a contemporary and explanatory metaphor can be extracted. For example, the large, controlling, clearly visible, highly formal and rationally organized military forces of the "Coalition" in the twenty-first-century war in Afghanistan represent, and have, a *strategy,* and are facing a disparate, unpredictable network of *tactics* employed by militant groups who are themselves outnumbered and outgunned, but able to operate "invisibly" precisely due to their relative lack of power. The British and Americans have established military bases, supply lines and prisons, literal sites of coordination and embodiment from which "targets and threats" can be identified and managed and soldiers, missiles, security forces, polling stations, translators and (re)building contractors can be deployed. However, car bombings, roadside bombings and suicide bombings, kidnappings and the strike-and-run actions of the embedded hostile forces are proving an effective, albeit not winning, retaliation. The two sides are in effective stalemate, not because they are equally matched in terms of monetary and weaponry might, but because the American and British troops are simply too numerous and strong for the other to overthrow outright, and the insurgents are too dispersed and able to operate and retaliate within the vulnerable, yet not fatally so, "gaps" of the liberating/occupying industrial-war complex. They are dependent on one another in terms of their sustained presence, with the practices of each being unavoidably shaped and determined by those of the other.

As argued, and in light of the preceding discussions of "ambivalence" and "resistance," the cultural circuits' conceptualization of the spread of discursive networks of subjectification holds that many of the various integral elements are by their very nature often individually inconsistent, incoherent and contradictory to the whole; and, based on the above metaphor, de Certeau provides a way with which to effectively account for such variations in how strategies (or Agendas) are interpreted, appropriated and consumed by human agents:

> Although they use as their material the vocabularies of established languages (those of television, newspapers, the supermarket or city planning), although they remain within the framework of prescribed syntaxes (the temporal modes of schedules, paradigmatic organizations or places etc.), these "traverses" remain heterogeneous to the systems they infiltrate and in which they sketch out the guileful ruses of different interests and desires. They circulate, come and go, overflow and drift over an imposed terrain, like the snowy waves of the sea slipping in among the rocks and defiles of an established order.
>
> (de Certeau, 1988: 34)

Tactics are therefore responses to a strategy that exist within, operate upon and emerge from the inevitable spaces or gaps between the actants in its network and their connections. With its enduring multi-level realms and shocks, actors, objects and templates, myths, ideologies and crowning subject position of *Homo happicus* that collectively constitute the socio-cultural endeavor to politicize, scientize and individualize happiness, the Agenda is then plainly describable as a *strategy,* while the immeasurable occurrences of contextual, idiosyncratic interpretations, adoptions, comportments, avoidances, alterations and rejections are indicative of the essentially human reactionary *tactics* employed within it.

A happy strategy

Notably, despite the antagonistic imagery taken from the above example of the Afghanistan war and de Certeau in his presentation of how they operate in relation to one another, tactics do not by default have to be attempts to damage or destroy the strategy that surrounds them. It is a collective term for the human employments and reactions generated, be they "ambivalent" attempts to embrace or subvert, but that in certain contexts are represented as hostile. Recalling Figure 1.1 on p. 44, by way of example, all of the objects and practices within the *Distribution* column are interpretive translations of the over-arching Happiness Agenda (or strategy), that emanates from the *Ideological Shocks*, made and performed by the actors located within the *Information Generating* column. These can consist of: television documentaries, newspaper and magazine articles, and books (including this one) that explore happiness either laudatory or critically; political debates which contest the ability to measure or affect the happiness of a populace; and corporate wellness or SMD policies that aim in some way to either harness or merely facilitate it. All are considerable as tactics, which in varying fashions engage with the following tenets: that happiness is objectual, can be pursued through scientific reasoning, and turned into personal and corporate practice and legislation.

Some support and promote such contentions outright, while others, such as the representative *Grumpy Old Men* discussed above, are less proactive. All are independent and unique from one another, emphasizing different focal points, perspectives and conclusions, highlighting the manner in which such actors and objects are unavoidably influenced but not inescapably controlled by the "nexus" of the surrounding cultural circuits. They are then, whether benefactor or malefactor, all part of the "crusade" (recall Furedi, 2006b: 1) of happiness acting to contribute to the prominence of the overall strategy, and emblematic of the bespoke *uses* and *making do* implicit in agents' embedded "guileful ruses, interests and desires" (de Certeau, 1988: 34).

This commonality-underlying-diversity demonstrates then how human agency interacts with the widespread impulse of the Happiness Agenda in non-uniform ways and degrees, and recalls de Certeau's above definition of "resistance" through the articulation of *tactics* that operate within the "gaps" (de Certeau, 1988: 32). However, it also, as discussed above, exemplifies how difficult it is to operate exclusively *without* the Agenda due its infusion with the backdrop of modernity. So, while the notion of the human agent not being merely *either* entirely overly socialized *or* a cultural dupe is of course hardly novel in social science and organizational sociology and research (cf. Scott, 1998; Thompson and McHugh, 2002; Sayer, 2007), the manner of conceiving of and understanding the complexities of human activities, interactions and practices through this model of theorizing, in relation to personal, political and organizational realities influenced by the extraordinary discursive apparatus (recall Thrift, 2005b: 6) of the circulation of happiness throughout the Anglo-American world, appears to offer a less-trodden path through old ground. As Reed infers, "the 'agency/structure debate' refuses to lie down"; and a practice- and appropriation-based approach provides fresh possible answers to: "questions about the nature of and link between human agency and its contexts" (2000: 45).

Ultimately, this kind of analysis nullifies the validity of promoting and maintaining oppositional theoretical constructs that collapse insight into human agency as being indicative of, say, "resistance *or* control," and highlights actual human practice, how and why it occurs and relates to the wider socio-cultural environment at the level of individual "use." From this amalgamated perspective, it can be inferred that there is unavoidably always space for humanity to express itself within social and discursive apparatus, rendering enactment with the Happiness Agenda as occurring in a spectrum of shades rather than opposing totalities. As de Certeau infers, we are "unrecognized producers who discover our own paths" in the "jungles" of the modern era (de Certeau, 1988: xviii). The contextually-influenced and personalized *consumption* of the Agenda, by human agents attempting to be happy through the inter-relating mediums of politics, organizations and personal action, is thus not only possible, but arguably both inevitable and vital to its contemporary sustainment.

7
Happy ever after?

All great truths begin as blasphemies.

(Shaw, 2008: 20)

As perhaps with any prolonged contemplation of the present, a slight expectancy befalls the final comments to speculate upon how developments currently in fruition might ultimately play out. There are then two principal avenues of potential progress resulting from this book which should be, at least briefly, deliberated upon, the first of which pertains to proactive and actionable advisements for future study. This overall account is, admittedly and even necessarily, unconventional in terms of its structure and approach to research. The primary intention here has been to identify and expose the Happiness Agenda, and to show how it can be understood and ana-lyzed. Having addressed such a task, subsequent efforts could focus on specific occurrences in greater depth, in contrast to the attempts here to demonstrate the breadth, variance and multi-dimensionality of the processes under investigation.

The notion of happiness has been used throughout this body of work to examine to validity of viewing the world through this metatheoretical lens of rhizomatic networks of heterogeneous actors and objects that construct compelling but not rigid subject positions for consumption by willing human agents. There is, however, ample reason to believe other mass-discursive, cultural phenomenon could also be understood is such terms. While much of what has been argued regards contemporary Anglo-American attempts to be happy, the explanatory model employed is itself much larger and has other possibilities. Thrift performs similar activity with his work on capitalism, and also complexity theory, but the investigation of movements such as religions, both New Age and traditional, and even particular organizational prerogatives could also be engaged in.

This might lead to further discussions regarding the notion of political, organizational and personal governance, as each inevitably impacts upon the others, and all are central to the functioning of society. As already detailed at length, happiness has recently been embraced as a way of ordering the modern Anglo-American world, which has repercussions for both practice and study in organizational settings. Considering it in more depth in terms of how corporate governance is yielded and put into effect would likely produce interesting analyses of the sites, nature and effects of power and subjectification in workplaces. If corporations have the ability, and right, to cater for and provide personal happiness, well-being and self-development to those within their employ, this arguably affords them a significant degree of authority and influence; for what they can provide they can also rescind. To return to the spiritualistic overtones of the current embodiment of happiness, this then epitomizes a substantial corporate appropriation of core elements of an individual's life, which is exponentially complicated by the environmental, macro-economic pressures exerted upon all firms. In the wake of financial downturns, the deeply personal, individualized and morally defensible pursuit of happiness can, paradoxically, be derailed by factors out of the individual's control. Redundancy, for example, may then result in the loss of more than merely monetary income, but also a primary means of one's ability to be happy. The occurrence and impacts of this offer another direction of investigation to scholars that would render an array of intriguing and worthwhile results.

Finally, one certainty is that with the sheer volume of orthodox scientistic, rationalist and instrumentalist research, often intended to deliberately and proactively improve organizations and society, dominating the cultural channels of the Happiness Agenda, there is a perpetual scholarly need to retain a purposeful monitoring, in order to assess, and if necessary inject, reflexivity and methodological awareness and balance. Modern corporations and governments are seemingly very much seduced by scientific-sounding, evidence-based data that can lead directly to the establishment of new policies and best-practice initiatives. This is demonstrative of the shift between *Mode 1* and *Mode 2* knowledge generation, as shown by Nowotny, Scott and Gibbons:

> The old paradigm of scientific discovery (Mode 1) characterized by the hegemony of disciplinary science, with its strong sense of internal hierarchy between the disciplines and driven by the autonomy of scientists and their host institutions, the universities, was being superseded – although not replaced – by a new paradigm of knowledge production (Mode 2), which was socially distributed, application-oriented, transdisciplinary, and subject to multiple accountabilities.
>
> (2005: 39)

The research strategies of Mode 1 typically have "little interest in application" (van Aken, 2001: 3), and Mode 2 seems to represent the battery of political, academic and organizational disciplines engrossed with how happiness can be found, measured, improved and applied. While there is indeed potentially great benefit in such actions, care should though be taken to avoid a descent into *operationism* (recall Allport, cited in Hall and Lindzey, 1960: 260).

This was the caveat of Gordon Allport who, as outlined in Chapter 4, despite retaining an interest in how the findings of psychological experiments could be related to an "action setting," was perturbed by sweeping "borrowing" of methods from the natural sciences. Operationism was imported from physics in the 1930s, an act which has been lambasted by many, including its founder, the physicist P.W. Bridgman, as "unworkable" and "misunderstood" by certain psychologists: "its continued presence in psychology is well-nigh scandalous and indicated a shoddy level of scholarship" (Grace, 2001: 7). Described as a positivist approach, in which "publicly observable sets of procedures" are necessarily utilized to "manipulate or measure a variable," in order to render research meaningful (ibid.: 5–6), it is a concerted, even intractable, attempt to find the "measurement operations" of each and every empirical concept (recall again Hall and Lindzey, 1960: 260) whether or not they may actually exist, rather than a focus on observation and understanding.

Grace determines that the *failure* of those committed to operationism was their "uncritical acceptance of mechanistic explanations, and, especially, in their belief that a single operation constituted a valid scientific definition for an observable construct" (2001: 7). It is important that the current expanse of advocates of the measurability and applicability of happiness are not permitted to descend into such mind frames, although it could be contended some already are, as may be incurred by a large-scale replacement of qualitative understanding with that which is predominantly quantitative. A balance struck between the two that welcomes but does not demand a translation between investigation and recommendation would provide greater validity and benefit to all concerned.

The second avenue of consideration is far more speculative and concerns the obsessions of society to come. This recalls the truism that as a sentient, reflective and introspective species, overly and uniquely consumed with studying ourselves, humanity is always unavoidably progressing through time and social change, left contemplating upon that which was once contemporary, be it a few seconds or several years back hence. Therefore, that which is so central, accepted and culturally pervasive today will inevitably be at some point confined to the annals of history. There are very few socially produced, "decisive shifts" which have occurred that will or cannot ever fall victim to change (Thrift, 2005g: 112). If anything, it is possible that the sacralization of the self will leave a legacy of its novel forms of expression and agency enduring into the future, as they have been substantial enough to usurp (some of) our conceptualizations of external gods, but even these should not be extended any guarantee of indelibility.

To borrow from George Bernard Shaw's above introductory quote, the final "blasphemy" of this work is then the unashamed profanity that the secularized, hedonic *faith* of Happiness, having reigned for circa three hundred years since the periods of Enlightenment and industrialization, is a peculiar ideological, culturally, politically and organizationally maintained construct, which is neither necessarily timeless nor natural to Anglo-Americans in an evolutionary or physiological sense, or indeed even so to all humans throughout the globe now. It succeeded the ideologies of before, and will be so succeeded by those to come. It is then, to repeat that stated in the Introduction, rather akin to a *Potemkin Village*: a *façade* that lacks the permanence implied by the very complexity of its production. It is a "learned" preoccupation that has been rendered "perfectly explicit, conscious and socially acceptable" (recall Miller, 1964: 289), rather than an inevitable, ever-present and universal anxiety.

However, to preserve a sense of "qualified optimism," as advised by Parker (2002: 47), this is, again, not to suggest that any of the attempts to find, provide or increase happiness, well-being, positivity and spirituality, or the ideas on which they are based, are in any way *fake*, *bad* or *wrong*. They certainly have many potent and often beneficial effects. The Agenda is only a façade in the manner in which its processes and practices of political, organizational and psychological production mask the fact that it is essentially discursive (as defined in Chapter 1) in origin, maintenance and circulation, which imply that it resonates with an enduring inevitability throughout the collective past, present and future of human existence.

The politicized and organized desire for happiness, as it is manifest today in its many, many guises, is not then a concern of the human agent beyond the influence of inevitable temporal and sociological progression: Tony Soprano's obsessive compulsion with finding it will not always make so much sense. To recall Herzberg, when the theoretical and mythic foundations that support *the pursuit of happiness* erode, the entire edifice will come tumbling down. The legions of broadcasters, publishers, economists, politicians, judges, companies, comedians and citizens *et al.* discussing it now will likely one day be as equally interested in (an)other phenomenon, which will become elevated and reified to a similar status of being a "natural" anxiety of humankind, as is currently bestowed upon the interpretation of and desire to *be happy*. What this, or they, will be exactly is, however, impossible to say, and can only be speculated upon and awaited with interest.

The strength of the Happiness Agenda, the sheer multitude and re-production of its diverse and even competing tactics, actors, objects and templates that feed its circulation, its very *performativity*, will then be its downfall. The inherent fragility and the often contradictory and "ambivalent" nature of the alliance and translations between actants will ultimately, cumulatively, exert a collective pressure towards the embrace of other pronounced discursive shifts that will subvert and undermine the hegemonies of today. Perhaps the fledgling seeds of such change can already be seen in the various criticisms of: positive psychology's mythical foundations and rejection of its ancestry, the human relations assumption in a causal link between employee happiness and productivity, and utilitarian attempts to produce a calculus of felicity.

The society-wide employment of tactics that keeps the balance towards maintaining the Agenda will eventually provide new influential theoretical advances or *shocks* and culturally and politically accepted ideas and practices, with a novel and consistent direction. Ideologies centered around: patriotism, terrorism (or the war on it), enhanced environmentalism, a *de*-individualized *neo*-socialism, resurgent fundamentalist religious beliefs, the advanced exploration of the solar system, or even movements attempting to foster a form of One World-ism, or its counterpart, "global civil war" (Agamben, 2005: 2), all of which are already varyingly prominent, may be seized and embodied in cultural artefacts and legislative and corporate templates; possibly becoming essentially defining concerns and producing subject positions for future humanity (in Anglo-American society or wherever) to collectively see and comport themselves and, repeating an earlier used phrase, *wrap their lives around*.

The fragments that make up our existence will thus inevitably shift, given a long enough timescale, but due to their nature many of these transitions will arguably be relatively subtle so as to escape much of but the most deliberate of focus; the changes influenced by the advent of the utilitarianism, human relations and positivity movements, for example, did not occur instantly, until one day the purposefully individualist, humanist, rationalist and instrumentalist strive to be happy is little more than a cultural quirk of a bygone age. As the "we" of some future present look back on the "us" of now—as we may reflect upon past societies' beliefs in, say, human sacrifice, self-flagellation or worshiping of the Sun—what they will see of our contemporaneous social norms will likely seem most peculiar and strange. Karl Marx once said "all that is solid melts into air, all that is holy is profaned," and the modern obsession with happiness, as naturalized, complex and culturally imbedded as it is, is no exception.

LIBRARY, UNIVERSITY OF CHESTER

References

Abner, M. (1997) "Corporate America Takes Fun Seriously," *Women in Business*, 49(5): 42.

Ackroyd, S. (2002) *The Organization of Business: Applying Organizational Theory to Contemporary Change*, Oxford: Oxford University Press.

Ackroyd, S. and Collinson, D. (2004) "Resistance, Misbehaviour and Dissent," in Ackroyd, S., Batt, R., Thompson, P. and Tolbert P.S. (eds.) *The Oxford Handbook of Work and Organization*, Oxford: Oxford University Press.

Agamben, G. (2005) *State of Exception*, Chicago: University of Chicago Press.

Aristotle (350 BCE, republished in 2009) Book 1.9, "The Human Good," in *The Nicomachean Ethics*, (trans. D. Ross), New York: Oxford University Press Inc.

Armstrong, P. (2001) "Styles of Illusion," in *The Sociology Review*, Malden, MA: Blackwell.

Babington, D. (2007) "Americans Less Happy Today Than 30 Years Ago: Study," *Reuters Online,* June 15, available at: http://www.reuters.com/article/idUSL155030 9820070615, accessed May 12th, 2010.

Bakan, J. (2004) *The Corporation: The Pathological Pursuit of Profit and Power*, London: Constable.

Barley, S.R. and Kunda, G. (1992) "Design and Devotion: Surges of Rational and Normative Ideologies of Control in Managerial Discourse," *Administrative Science Quarterly*, 37(3): 363–99.

Barnes, B. (2001) "Practices as Collective Action in Theory," in Schatzki, T., Knorr-Cetina, K. and Von Savigny, E. (eds.) *The Practice Turn in Contemporary Theory*, London: Routledge.

Bell, E. and Taylor, S. (2004) "From Outward Bound to Inward Bound: The Prophetic Voices and Discursive Practices of Spiritual Management Development", *Human Relations*, 57(4): 439–66.

Bentham, J. (1996), cited in Burns, J.H. and Hart, H.L.A. (eds.) *The Collected Works of Jeremy Bentham: An Introduction to the Principles of Morals and Legislation*, Oxford: Clarendon Press.

Bernstein, S.D. (2006) "Positive Organizational Scholarship: Meet the Movement: An Interview with Kim Cameron, Jane Dutton, and Robert Quinn," *Journal of Management Enquiry*, 12(3): 266–71.

Best and Worst Places to Live (2005–2007) a property information programme, Channel 4.

Blackler, F. (2004a) "Understanding Practices, Managing Changes," Lectures given at Trento University, session 2.

Blackler, F. (2004b) "Understanding Practices, Managing Changes," Lectures given at Trento University, session 2.

Blackler, F. and Regan, S. (2005) "The Conflicted Object: Strategy as Organisational Practice," Lectures given at Trento University, session 2.

Bloomfield, B.P. (1995) "Power, Machines and Social Relations: Delegating to Information Technology in the UK National Health Service," *Organization*, 2(3/4): 489–518.

Bloomfield, B. and Vurdubakis, T. (2002) "The Vision Thing: Constructing Technology and the Future in Management Advice," in Clark, T. and Fincham, R. (eds.) *Critical Consulting: New Perspectives on the Management Advice Industry*, Oxford: Blackwell Business.

Boltanksi, L. and Chiapello, E. (2005) *The New Spirit of Capitalism*, New York: Verso.

Bolton, S.C. (2000) "Emotion Here, Emotion There, Emotional Organisations Everywhere," *Critical Perspectives on Accounting*, 11: 155–71.

Bolton, S.C. and Boyd, C. (2003) "Trolley Dolly or Skilled Emotion Manager? Moving on from Hochschild's Managed Heart," *Work, Employment and Society*, 17: 289–308.

Bos, R.T. (2000) *Fashion and Utopia in Management Thinking*, Philadelphia, PA: John Benjamins.

Bretherton, R. and Ørner, R. (2003) "Positive Psychotherapy in Disguise," *The Psychologist*, 16(3): 136–7.

Briner, B. (2001) *The Management Methods of Jesus: Ancient Wisdom for Modern Business*, Nashville, TN: Thomas Nelson Publishers.

Brooker, C. (2001) *TV Go Home*, London: Fourth Estate.

Brooker, C. (2007) *Dawn of the Dumb: Dispatches from the Idiotic Frontline*, London: Faber and Faber.

Brooks, D. (2000) *Bobos in Paradise: The New Upper Class and How They Got There*, New York: Simon & Schuster.

Brown, D. (1971) *Bury My Heart at Wounded Knee: An Indian History of the American West*, New York: Rinehart & Winston.

Brubaker, R. (1984) *The Limits of Rationality: An Essay on the Social and Moral Thought of Max Weber*, London: Allen and Unwin.

Burrell, G. (1988) "Modernism, Postmodernism and Organizational Analysis 2: The Case of Michel Foucault," *Organization Studies*, 9(2): 221–35.

Calás, M. and Smircich, L. (2003) "Introduction: Spirituality, Management and Organization," *Organization*, 10(2): 327–8.

Callon, M. (1991) "Techno-Economic Networks and Irreversibility," in Law, J. (ed.) *A Sociology of Monsters: Essays on Power, Technology and Domination*, London and New York: Routledge.

Cameron, D. (2010) on *BBC News Politics*, 25 November, available at: http://www.bbc.co.uk/news/uk-11833241, accessed 25 November, 2010.

Cameron, K.S. and Caza, A. (2004) "Introduction: Contributions to the Discipline of Positive Organizational Scholarship," *American Behavioral Scientist*, 47(6): 1–9.

Chaiklin, S. and Lave, J. (1993) *Understanding Practice: Perspectives on Activity and Context*, Cambridge: Cambridge University Press.

Chesney, M.A., Darbes, A., Hoerster, K., Taylor, J.M., Chambers, D.B. and Anderson, D.E. (2005) "Positive Emotions: Exploring the Other Hemisphere in Behavioral Medicine," *International Journal of Behavioral Medicine*, 12(2): 50–8.

Chia, R. (2004) "Strategy-as-practice: Reflections on the Research Agenda," *European Management Review*, 1: 29–34.

CIPD (Chartered Institute of Personnel Development) (2007) "Public Policy Perspectives Document 'Smart Work'," available at: www.cipd.co.uk, accessed 23 July 2009.

CIPD website, all information garnered from www.cipd.co.uk/, accessed 4 October 2010.

Clark, T. and Salaman, G. (1998) "Telling Tales: Management Gurus' Narratives and the Construction of Managerial Identity," *Journal of Management Studies*, 35(2): 137–61.

Clough, P. and Nutbrown, C. (2002) *A Student's Guide to Methodology*, London: Sage.

Cooley, M. (1980) *Architect or Bee? The Human/Technology Relationship*, Boston: South End Press.

Cooper, R. and Burrell, G. (1988) "Modernism, Postmodernism and Organizational Analysis: An Introduction," *Organization Studies*, 9(1): 91–112.

Currie, G. and Knights, D. (2003) "Reflecting on a Critical Pedagogy in MBA Education", *Management Learning*, 34(1): 27–49.

Damasio, A.R. (1998) "Emotion in the Perspective of an Integrated Nervous System," *Brain Research Reviews*, 26: 83–6.

Dawkins, R. (2006) *The God Delusion*, London: Bantam Press.

de Certeau, M. (1988) *The Practice of Everyday Life*, Berkeley, CA: University of California Press.

de Laet, M. and Mol, A. (2000) "The Zimbabwe Bush Pump: Mechanics of a Fluid Technology," *Social Studies of Science*, 30(2): 225–63.

Deleuze, G. and Guattari, F. (1988) *A Thousand Plateaus: Capitalism and Schizophrenia*, London: Athlone Press.

Diener, E. Lucas, R.E. and Oishi, S. (2005) "Subjective Well-being: The Science of Happiness and Life Satisfaction," in Snyder, C.R. and Lopez, S.J. (eds.) *Handbook of Positive Psychology*, Oxford: Oxford University Press.

Diken, B. (1998) *Strangers, Ambivalence and Social Theory*, Aldershot: Ashgate.

Duncan, G. (2007) "After Happiness," *Journal of Political Ideologies*, 12(1): 85–108.

Easton, M. (2006a) "Britain's Happiness in Decline," BBC News Online, 3 April, available at: http://news.bbc.co.uk/1/hi/programmes/happiness_formula/4771908.stm, accessed 13 July 2007.

Easton, M. (2006b) *The Happiness Formula*, BBC2 documentary, aired in Britain between 3 May 2006 and 7 June 2006.

Edmonds, N. (2006) "How to Be Positively Happy," *Daily Mail*, 24 July, pp. 26–8.

Ehrenreich, B. (2006) *Bait and Switch: The Futile Pursuit of the Corporate Dream*, London: Granta Books.

Elliott, T.R., Kurylo, M. and Rivera, P. (2005) "Positive Growth Following Acquired Physical Disability," in Snyder, C.R. and Lopez, S.J. (eds.) *Handbook of Positive Psychology*, Oxford: Oxford University Press.

Ellul, J. (1964) *The Technological Society*, New York: Vintage Books.

Evans, D. (2002) *Emotion: The Science of Sentiment*, Oxford: Oxford University Press.

Feldman, F. (1997) *Utilitarianism, Hedonism, and Desert: Essays in Moral Philosophy*, Cambridge: Cambridge University Press.

Ferguson, I. (2006) "Richard Layard, Inequality and the 'Science' of Happiness", *Socialist Worker*, 9 December, issue 2030.

Fincham, R. and Clark, T. (2002) "Introduction: The Emergence of Critical Perspectives on Consulting," in Clark, T. and Fincham, R. (eds.) *Critical Consulting: New Perspectives on the Management Advice Industry*, Oxford: Blackwell Business.

Fineman, S. (2006) "On Being Positive: Concerns and Counterpoints," *The Academy of Management Review*, 31(2): 270–91.

Fisher, C.D. (1980) "On the Dubious Wisdom of Expecting Job Satisfaction to Correlate with Performance," *The Academy of Management Review*, 5(4): 607–12.

Fisher, C.D. (2003) "Why Do Lay People Believe that Satisfaction and Performance Are Correlated? Possible Sources of a Commonsense Theory," *Journal of Organizational Behavior*, 24: 753–77.

Flora, P. (1985) "Major Problems and Dimensions of the Welfare State," in Eisenstadt, S.N. and Ahimeir, O. (eds.) *The Welfare State and Its Aftermath*, Worcester: Billing and Sons Limited.

Fleming, P. and Sewell, G. (2002) "Looking for the Good Soldier, Švejk: Alternative Modalities of Resistance in the Contemporary Workplace," *Sociology*, 36(4): 857–73.

Foucault, M. (1991) *Discipline and Punish: The Birth of the Prison*, London: Penguin.

Fredrickson, B.L. (2003) "The Emerging Science of Positive Psychology is Coming to Understand Why it's Good to Feel Good," *American Scientist*, 91: 330–5.

Fukuyama, F. (1992) *The End of History and the Last Man*, London: Penguin.

Furedi, F. (2006a) "Why the 'Politics of Happiness' Makes Me Mad," *Spiked*, 23 May, available at: http://www.spiked-online.com/index.php/site/article/311/, accessed 21 March 2007.

Furedi, F. (2006b) "Politicians, Economists, Teachers...Why Are They So Desperate to Make Us Happy?," *The Telegraph Online*, 7 May, available at: http://www.Telegraph.co.uk/opinion/main.jhtml?xml=/opinion/2006/05/07/do0706.xml&sSheet=/portal/2006/05/07/ixportal.html, accessed 22 March 2007.

Furusten, S. (1999) *Popular Management Books: How They Are Made and What They Mean for Organizations*, London: Routledge.

Fusaro, P.C. and Miller, R.M. (2002) *What Went Wrong at Enron?*, New Jersey: Wiley.

Gable, S. and Haidt, J. (2005) "What (and Why) is Positive Psychology?," *Review of General Psychology*, 9(2): 103–10.

Galbraith, J.K. (1996) *The Good Society: The Humane Agenda*, London: Sinclair-Stevenson.

Gillespie, R. (1991) *Manufacturing Knowledge: A History of the Hawthorne Experiments*, Cambridge: Cambridge University Press.

Goldsmith, B. (2003) "Fun Adds Up," *Successful Meetings*, 52(7): 26.

Goleman, D. (1996) *Emotional Intelligence: Why it Can Matter More Than IQ*, London: Bloomsbury.

Goodchild, P. (1996) *Deleuze and Guattari: An Introduction to the Politics of Desire*, London: Sage.

Goodin, R.E. and Dryzek, J. (1987) "Risk-sharing and Social Justice: The Motivational Foundations of the Post-War Welfare State," in Gooden, R.E. and Le Grand, J. (eds.) *Not Only the Poor: The Middle Classes and the Welfare State*, London: Allen & Unwin.

Grace, R.C. (2001) "On the Failure of Operationism," *Theory and Psychology*, 11(5): 4–33.

Gray, J. (2002) *False Dawn: The Delusions of Global Capitalism*, London: Granta Books.

Green, G. (1975) *The End of the Affair*, Harmondsworth: Penguin.

Greer, P. (1994) *Transforming Central Government: The Next Steps Initiative*, Buckingham: Open University Press.

Grey, C. (2005) *A Very Short, Fairly Interesting and Reasonably Cheap Book about Studying Organizations*, London: Sage Publications.

Grumpy Old Men (2003–2006) a talking head panel programme, BBC.

Grumpy Old Women (2005–2008) a talking head panel programme, BBC.

Grumpy Young Men (2009) a talking head panel programme, Paramount Comedy.

Guest, D.E. (1987) "Human Resource Management and Industrial Relations," *Journal of Management Studies*, 24(5): 503–21.

Guest, D.E. (1990) "Human Resource Management and the American Dream," *Journal of Management Studies*, 27(4): 377–97.

Hall, C.S. and Lindzey, G. (1960) *Theories of Personality*, 6th edn, New York: John Wiley & Sons Inc.

Handelsman, M.M., Knapp, S. and Gottleib, M.C. (2005) "Positive Ethics," in Snyder, C.R. and Lopez, S.J. (eds.) *Handbook of Positive Psychology*, Oxford: Oxford University Press.

Heelas, P. (1992) "The Sacralization of the Self in New Age Capitalism," in Abercrombie, N. and Warde, A. (eds.) *Social Change in Contemporary Britain*, Cambridge: Polity Press.

Heelas, P. (1996) *The New Age Movement*, Oxford: Blackwell.

Heelas, P. (2002) "Work Ethics, Soft Capitalism and the "Turn to Life'," in Du Gay, P. and Pryke, M. (eds.) *Cultural Economy: Cultural Analysis and Commercial Life*, London: Sage.

Heisenberg, W. (2009) cited in Haisch, B. *The God Theory: Universes, Zero-Point Fields, and What's Behind It All*, San Francisco: Red Wheel/Weiser LLC.

Held, B.S. (2004) "The Negative Side of Positive Psychology," *Journal of Applied Humanistics*, 44: 9–46.

Helzberg Jr., B. (2005) "Customer Service," *American Salesman*, September, 50(9): 21.

Hendrick, S. and Hendrick, C. (2005) "Love," in Snyder, C.R. and Lopez, S.J. (eds.) *Handbook of Positive Psychology*, Oxford: Oxford University Press.

Henry, J. (2003) "Positive Organisations," *The Psychologist*, 16(3): 138–9.

Herzberg, F. (1972) *Work and the Nature of Man*, London: Staples Press.

Hicks, B. (1992) *Relentless* (DVD), Montreal: Rykodisc.

Hill, C. (1996) *Liberty Against the Law: Some Seventeenth-Century Controversies*, London: The Penguin Press.

Hill, J. (2003) "Bleak Future or New Dawn?," *The Psychologist*, 16(3): 137–8.

Hochschild, A.R. (1998) "The Sociology of Emotion as a Way of Seeing," in Bendelow, G.B. and Williams, S.J. (eds.) *Emotions in Social Life: Critical Themes and Contemporary Issues*, London: Routledge.

Hoffman, P. (2002) *The Wisdom of Crocodiles*, London: Black Swan.

Hollway, W. (1991) *Work Psychology and Organizational Behaviour: Managing the Individual Worker*, London: Sage Publications.

Hutton, W. (1996) *The State We're In*, London: Vintage.

Hutton, W. (2002) *The World We're In*, London: Time Warner Books.

Iaffaldano, M.T. and Muchinsky, P.M. (1985) "Job Satisfaction and Performance: A Meta Analysis," *Psychological Bulletin*, 97(2): 251–73.

Jackson, B. (2003) *Management Gurus and Management Fashions*, New York: Routledge.

Jackson, R. (2001) *Plato: A Beginner's Guide*, London: Hodder and Stoughton.

Jordison, S. and Kieran, D. (2003) *Crap Towns: The 50 Worst Places to Live in the UK*, vol. 1, London: Boxtree Ltd.

Jordison, S. and Kieran, D. (2004) *Crap Towns: The 50 Worst Places to Live in the UK*, vol. 2, London: Boxtree Ltd.

Judge, T.A., Thorensen, C.J., Bono, J.E. and Patton, G.K. (2001) "The Job Satisfaction-Job Performance Relationship: A Qualitative and Quantitative Review," *Psychological Bulletin*, 127(3): 376–407.

Kaufman, F. (1985) "Major Problems and Dimensions of the Welfare State," in Eisenstadt, S.N. and Ahimeir, O. (eds.) *The Welfare State and its Aftermath*, Worcester: Billing & Sons Limited.

Keay, D. (1987) interview with Margaret Thatcher for *Women's Own*, 23 September, available at:www.margaretthatcher.org/speeches/displaydocument.asp?docid=106689, accessed 3 October 2009.

Keyes, C.L.M. and Lopez, S.J. (2005) "Toward a Science of Mental Health: Positive Directions in Diagnosis and Interventions," in Snyder, C.R. and Lopez, S.J. (eds.) *Handbook of Positive Psychology*, Oxford: Oxford University Press.

Kieran, D. (2004) *Crap Jobs*, London: Bantam Books.

Kieran, D. (2005) *Crap Holidays*, London: Bantam Books.

Knorr-Cetina, K. (2001) "Objectual Practice in Theory," in Schatzki, T., Knorr-Cetina, K. and Von Savigny, E. (eds.) *The Practice Turn in Contemporary Theory*, London: Routledge.

Kosmala, K. (2006) "The Ambivalence of Professional Identity: On Cynicism and Jouissance in Audit Firms", *Human Relations*, 59(10): 1393–428.

Kurke, L.B. (2004) *The Wisdom of Alexander the Great: Enduring Leadership Lessons from the Man Who Created an Empire*, New York: AMACOM.

Latour, B. (1992) "Where Are the Missing Masses? Sociology of a Few Mundane Artifacts," in Bijker, J. and Law, J. (eds.) *Shaping Technology, Building Society: Studies in Sociotechnical Change*, Cambridge, MA: MIT Press.

Latour, B. (1993) *We Have Never Been Modern*, Hemel Hempstead: Harvester Wheatsheaf.

Latour, B. (1999) "On Recalling ANT," in Law, J. and Hassard, J. (eds.) *Actor Network and After*, Oxford: Blackwell.

Law, J. (1990) "Notes on the Theory of the Actor-Network," *Systems Practice*, 5(4): 379–93.

Layard, R. (2005) *Happiness: Lessons from a New Science*, London: Penguin Books.

Leavitt, H.J. (1989) "Educating Our MBAs: On Teaching What We Haven't Taught," *California Management Review*, 31(3): 38–50.

Ledford Jr., G.E. (1999) "Happiness and Productivity Revisited," *Journal of Organizational Behavior*, 20(1): 25–30.

Legge, K. (2002) "On Knowledge, Business Consultants and the Selling of Total Quality Management," in Clark, T. and Fincham, R. (eds.) *Critical Consulting: New Perspectives on the Management Advice Industry*, Oxford: Blackwell Business.

Linley, P.A., Joseph, S. and Boniwell, I. (2003) "Positive Psychology," *The Psychologist*, 16(3): 126.

Long, B.S. and McLeod, E.A. (2006) "The Varying Conceptualizations of Spirituality at Work: A Review of the Research," *Social Responsibility*, 27(29): 56–68.

Luthans, F. and Youssef, C.M. (2004) "Human, Social, and Now Positive Psychological Capital Management: Investing in People for Competitive Advantage," *Organizational Dynamics*, 33(2): 143–60.

Luthans, F. and Youssef, C.M. (2007) "Emerging Positive Organizational Behavior," *Journal of Management*, 33: 321–49.

Maddux, J.E. (2005) "Stopping the 'Madness'," in Snyder, C.R. and Lopez, S.J. (eds.) *Handbook of Positive Psychology*, Oxford: Oxford University Press.

Mahoney, M.J. (2005) "Constructivism and Positive Psychology," in Snyder, C.R. and Lopez, S.J. (eds.) *Handbook of Positive Psychology*, Oxford: Oxford University Press.

Martin, L.H., Gutman, H. and Hutton, P.H. (eds.) (1988) *Technologies of the Self: A Seminar with Michel Foucault*, London: Tavistock.

Martin, M.W. (2007) "Happiness and Virtue in Positive Psychology", *Journal for the Theory of Social Behaviour*, 37(1): 89–103.

Marx, K. ([1888] 1985) *The Communist Manifesto*, Harmondsworth: Penguin Books.

Maslow, A.H. (1970) *Motivation and Personality,* 2nd edn, New York: Harper and Row Publishers.

Maslow, A.H. (1998) *Maslow on Management*, New York: John Wiley & Sons Inc.

Mayo, E. (1946) *The Human Problems of an Industrial Civilization*, 2nd edn, Cambridge, MA: The Murray Printing Company.

McArthur, A. and Lowe, S. (2006) *Is It Just Me Or Is Everything Just Shit?: The Encyclopaedia of Modern Life*, London: Time Warner Books.

Miller, G.A. (1964) *Psychology: The Science of Mental Life*, London: Hutchinson and Co. Ltd.

Miller, P. and O'Leary, T. (1987) "Accounting and the Governable Person," *Accounting, Organizations and Society*, 12(3): 235–65.

Miller, P. and O'Leary, T. (1989) "Hierarchies and American Ideals, 1900–1940," *Academy of Management Review*, 14(2): 250–65.

Mishra, R. (1984) *The Welfare State in Crisis*, Brighton: Harvester Press.

Munro, R. (1996) "Alignment and Identity Work: The Study of Accounts and Accountability," in Munro, R. and Mouritsen, J. (eds.) *Accountability: Power, Ethos and the Technologies of Managing*, London: International Thompson Business Press.

Nair, K. (1997) *A Higher Standard of Leadership: Lessons from the Life of Gandhi*, San Francisco: Berrett-Koehler Publishers.

Newswipe (2009–2010) British news review programme, BBC Four.

Nietzsche, F. (1974) *The Gay Science*, New York: Vintage Books.

Nowotny, H., Scott, P. and Gibbons, M. (2005) "Re-Thinking Science: Mode 2 in Societal Context," in Carayannis, E.G. and Campbell, D.F.J. (eds.) *Knowledge Creation, Diffusion, and Use in Innovation Networks and Knowledge Clusters*, New York: Praeger Publishers Inc.

O'Connor, E. (1999a) "Minding the Workers: The Meaning of 'Human' and 'Human Relations'," in Elton Mayo, *Organization*, 6: 223–246.

O'Connor, E. (1999b) "The Politics of Management Thought: A Case Study of the Harvard Business School and the Human Relations School," *Academy of Management Review*, 24(1): 117–31.

Oleson, V. and Bone, D. (1998) "Emotions in Rationalizing Organizations: Conceptual Notes from Professional Nursing in the USA," in Bendelow, G.B. and Williams, S.J. (eds.) *Emotions in Social Life: Critical Themes and Contemporary Issues*, New York: Routledge.

O'Neill, B. (2005) "Why Are We So Grumpy?," on *BBC News online*, Wednesday, 5 January, available at: http://news.bbc.co.uk/1/hi/magazine/4145681.stm.

Oswald, A.J. (2003) "How Much Do External Factors Affect Well-being?," *The Psychologist*, 16(3): 140–1.

Overskeid, G. (2002) "Psychological Hedonism and the Nature of Motivation: Bertrand Russell's Anhedonic Desires," *Philosophical Psychology*, 15(1): 77–93.

Owen, G. (1999) *From Empire to Europe: The Decline and Revival of British Industry Since the Second World War*, London: HarperCollins.

Parker, M. (2002) *Against Management: Organization in the Age of Managerialism*, Cambridge: Polity Press.

Patton, P. (2006) "Order, Exteriority and Flat Multiplicities in the Social," in Fuglsang, M. and Sørensen, B.M. (eds.) *Deleuze and the Social*, Edinburgh: Edinburgh University Press.

Pea, R.D. and Brown, J.S. (1993) "Foreword," in Chaiklin, S. and Lave, J. (eds.) *Understanding Practice: Perspectives on Activity and Context*, Cambridge: Cambridge University Press.

Peters, T. (1987) *Thriving on Chaos: Handbook for a Management Revolution*, London: Pan.

Peters, T. and Waterman, R.H. (1982) *In Search of Excellence: Lessons from America's Best-Run Companies*, London: HarperCollins.

Petty, M.M., McGee, G.W. and Cavender, J.W. (1984) "A Meta-Analysis of the Relationships between Individual Job Satisfaction and Individual Performance," *The Academy of Management Review*, 9(4): 712–21.

Pfeffer, J. and Fong, C.T. (2004) "The Business School 'Business': Some Lessons from the US Experience," *Journal of Management Studies*, 41(8): 1501–20.

Plato (380 BCE, republished in 1994) *The Republic* (trans. D. Lee), London: Penguin.

Positive Organizational Scholarship website, all information garnered from www.bus.umich.edu/positive/, accessed 9 October 2010.

Positive Psychology website, all information garnered from www.ppc.sas.upenn.edu/index.html and www.authentichappiness.sas.upenn.edu/, accessed 12 July 2009.

Ramsey, R.D. (2001) "Fun at Work: Lessons from the Fish Market," *Supervision*, 62(4): 7.

Rasiel, E.M. (2000) *The McKinsey Way: Using the Techniques of the World's Top Strategic Consultants to Help You and Your Business*, New York: McGraw-Hill.

Reed, M.I. (2000) "In Praise of Duality and Dualism: Rethinking Agency and Structure in Organisational Analysis," in Ackroyd, S. and Fleetwood, S. (eds.) *Realist Perspectives on Management and Organisations*, New York: Routledge.

Resnick, S., Warmoth, A. and Serlin, I.A. (2001) "The Humanistic Psychology and Psychology Connection: Implications for Psychotherapy," *Journal of Humanistic Psychology*, 41: 73–101.

Roberts, L.M. (2006) "Response: Shifting the Lens on Organizational Life: The Added Value of Positive Scholarship," *Academy of Management Review*, 31(2): 292–305.

Roberts, M.C., Brown, K.J., Johnston, R.J. and Reinke, J. (2005) "Positive Psychology for Children: Development, Prevention, and Promotion," in Snyder, C.R. and Lopez, S.J. (eds.) *Handbook of Positive Psychology*, Oxford: Oxford University Press.

Rose, E. (2004) *Employment Relations*: *Continuity and Change*: *Policies and Practices*, London: Prentice Hall.

Rose, N. (1990) *Governing the Soul: The Shaping of the Private Self*, London: Free Association Books.

Rosen, F. (1996) "Introduction," in Burns, J.H. and Hart, H.L.A. (eds.) *The Collected Works of Jeremy Bentham: An Introduction to the Principles of Morals and Legislation*, Oxford: Clarendon Press.

Rowlands, M. (2005) *Everything I Know I Learned from TV*, London: Ebury Press.

Ryff, C.D. and Singer, B. (2005) "From Social Structure to Biology: Integrative Science in Pursuit of Human Health and Well-Being," in Snyder, C.R. and Lopez, S.J. (eds.) *Handbook of Positive Psychology*, Oxford: Oxford University Press.

Sahlins, M. (1996) "The Sadness of Sweetness: The Native Anthropology of Western Cosmology," *Current Anthropology*, 37(3): 395–428.

Saint-Martin, D. (2000) *Building the New Managerialist State: Consultants and the Politics of Public Sector Reform in Comparative Perspective*, Oxford: Oxford University Press.

Saville, J. (1987) "The Origins of the Welfare State," in Loney, M., Boswell, D. and Clark, J. (eds.) *Social Policy and Social Welfare*, Milton Keynes: Open University Press.

Sayer, A. (2007) "Moral Economy and Employment," in Bolton, S. and Houlihan, M. (eds.) *Searching for the Human in Human Resource Management*, London: Palgrave.

Schatzki, T. (2001) "Introduction to Practice Theory," in Schatzki, T., Knorr-Cetina, K. and Savigny, E. (eds.) *The Practice Turn in Contemporary Theory*, London: Routledge.

Schatzki, T. (2002) *The Site of the Social: A Philosophical Account of the Constitution of Social Life and Change*, Pennsylvania, PA: University Press.

Schoch, R. (2006) "The Secrets of Happiness: Why the Ancients Hold the Key," *The Independent EXTRA* supplement, 17 March.

Scott, A. (1998) "Irrational Choice? On Freedom, Coercion and the Labour Contract," *Capital and Class*, 64: 119–30.

Screenwipe (2006-2008) British television review programme, BBC Four.

Seligman, M.E.P. (1975) *Helplessness: On Depression, Development, and Death*, New York: Henry Holt & Co.

Seligman, M.E.P. (1999) "The President's Address (Annual Report)," *American Psychologist*, 54(3): 126–7.

Seligman, M.E.P. (2003) "Positive Psychology: Fundamental Assumptions," *The Psychologist*, 16(3): 126–7.

Seligman, M.E.P. (2005) "Positive Psychology, Positive Prevention, and Positive Therapy," in Snyder, C.R. and Lopez, S.J. (eds.) *Handbook of Positive Psychology*, Oxford: Oxford University Press.

Seligman, M.E.P., Parks, A.C. and Steen, T. (2004) "A Balanced Psychology and a Full Life," *The Royal Society*, 359: 1379–81.

Sennett, R. (1999) *The Corrosion of Character: The Personal Consequences of Work in the New Capitalism*, New York: Norton.

Shaw, G.B. (2008) *Annajanska, the Bolshevik Empress*, San Diego: Icon.

Shenhav, Y. (1994) "Manufacturing Uncertainty and Uncertainty in Manufacturing: Managerial Discourse and the Rhetoric of Organization Theory," *Science in Context*, 13: 275–305.

Shenhav, Y. (2003) "Fusing Sociological Theory with Engineering Discourse: The Historical and Epistemological Foundations of Organization Theory," in Christian, K. and Tsoukas, H. (eds.) *The Oxford Handbook of Organization Theory: Meta-theoretical Perspectives*, Oxford: Oxford University Press.

Singleton, V. and Michael, M. (1993) "Actor-Networks and Ambivalence: General Practitioners in the UK Cervical Screening Programme," *Social Studies of Science*, 23(2): 227–64.

Sklair, L. (1995) *Sociology of the Global System*, Hemel Hempstead: Prentice-Hall.

Skirbekk, G. and Gilje, N. (2001) *A History of Western Thought: From Ancient Greece to the Twentieth Century*, 7th edn, London: Routledge.

Smail, D. (1993) *The Origins of Unhappiness: A New Understanding of Personal Distress*, Glasgow: HarperCollins.

Snyder, C.R. and Lopez, S.J. (eds.) (2005a) "Preface," in Snyder, C.R. and Lopez, S.J. (eds.) *Handbook of Positive Psychology*, Oxford: Oxford University Press.

Snyder, C.R. and Lopez, S.J. (2005b) "The Future of Positive Psychology: A Declaration of Independence," in Snyder, C.R. and Lopez, S.J. (eds.) *Handbook of Positive Psychology*, Oxford: Oxford University Press.

Starkey, K., Hatchuel, A. and Tempest, S. (2004) "Rethinking the Business School," *Journal of Management Studies*, 41(8): 1521–31.

Starkey, K. and Tempest, S. (2005) "The Future of the Business School: Knowledge Challenges and Opportunities," *Human Relations*, 58(1): 61–82.

Staw, B.M. (2003) "Organizational Psychology and the Pursuit of the Happy/ Productive Worker," in Porter, L.W., Bigley G.A. and Steers, R.M. (eds.) *Motivation and Work Behaviour*, 7th edn, New York: McGraw-Hill.

Stromberg, R.N. (1981) *European Intellectual History Since 1789*, Englewood Cliffs, NJ: Prentice Hall, Inc.

Taksa, L. (1992) "Scientific Management: Technique or Cultural Ideology?," *The Journal of Industrial Relations*, 34(3): 365–95.

Taksa, L. (1995) "The Cultural Diffusion of Scientific Management: The United States and New South Wales," *The Journal of Industrial Relations*, 37(3): 427–461.

Taylor, E. (2001) "Positive Psychology and Humanistic Psychology: A Reply to Seligman," *Journal of Humanistic Psychology*, 41: 13–29.

Taylor, F.W. (1947a) "Shop Management," in *Scientific Management*, 3rd edn, New York: Harper & Brothers Publishers.

Taylor, F.W. (1947b) "The Principles of Scientific Management," in *Scientific Management*, 3rd edn, New York: Harper & Brothers Publishers.

The Economist Online (2005) "Economics and Human Evolution," 7 April, available at: http://www.economist.com/science/displaystory.cfm?story_i d=3839749, accessed 17 September 2010.

The Sopranos (2002) *The Strong, Silent Type*, episode 4.10, fictional television programme about the Mafia, HBO, aired 17 December.

Thompson, P. (2003) "Disconnected Capitalism: Or Why Employers Can't Keep Their Side of the Bargain," *Work, Employment and Society*, 17: 359–78.

Thompson, P. and Ackroyd, S. (1995) "All Quiet on the Workplace Front? A Critique of Recent Trends in British Industrial Sociology," *Sociology*, 29(4): 615–33.

Thompson, P. and McHugh, D. (2002) *Work Organisations: A Critical Introduction*, New York: Palgrave.

Thrift, N. (1999) "The Place of Complexity," *Theory, Culture & Society*, 16(31): 30–69.

Thrift, N. (2001) "Forum: Perspectives on New Political Economy," *New Political Economy*, 6(3): 375–80.

Thrift, N. (2005a) *Knowing Capitalism*, London: Sage.

Thrift, N. (2005b) "Adventures of Capitalism," in *Knowing Capitalism*, London: Sage.

Thrift, N. (2005c) "The Rise of Soft Capitalism," in *Knowing Capitalism*, London: Sage.

Thrift, N. (2005d) "The Place of Complexity," in *Knowing Capitalism*, London: Sage.

Thrift, N. (2005e) "Virtual Capitalism: The Globalization of Reflexive Business Knowledge," in *Knowing Capitalism*, London: Sage.

Thrift, N. (2005f) "Cultures on the Brink: Re-engineering the Soul of Capitalism on a Global Scale," in *Knowing Capitalism*, London: Sage.

Thrift, N. (2005g) "It's the Romance, Not the Finance, that Makes the Business Worth Pursuing: Disclosing a New Market Culture," in *Knowing Capitalism*, London: Sage.

Thrift, N. (2005h) "Performing Cultures in the New Economy," in *Knowing Capitalism*, London: Sage.

Thrift, N. (2006) "Re-Inventing Invention: New Tendencies in Capitalist Commodification," *Economy and Society*, 35(2): 279–306.

Townley, B. (2002) "Managing with Modernity," *Organization*, 9(4): 549–73.

Toynbee, P. (2003) *Hard Work: Life in Low-Paid Britain*, London: Bloomsbury Publishing.

Turner, B.S. (2007) "Extended Review: Justification, the City and Late Capitalism," *The Sociological Review*, 55(2): 410–14.

Turner, N., Barling, J. and Zacharatos, A. (2005) "Positive Psychology at Work," in Snyder, C.R. and Lopez, S.J. (eds.) *Handbook of Positive Psychology*, Oxford: Oxford University Press.

van Aken, J.E. (2001) "Mode 2 Knowledge Production in the Field of Management," working paper, available at: http://64.233.179.104/scholar? hl=en&lr=&q=cache:QpU-lXicRc8J:fp.tm.tue.nl/ecis/working%2520papers/ eciswp46.pdf+nowotny+mode+one+knowledge, accessed 12 September 2010.

Veenhoven, R. (2003a) "Hedonism and Happiness," *Journal of Happiness Studies*, 4(4): 437–57.

Veenhoven, R. (2003b) "Happiness," *The Psychologist*, 16(3): 128–9.

Vroom, V.H. (1964) *Work and Motivation*, New York: Wiley.

Walker, A. (1994) "The Future of the British Welfare State: Privatisation or Socialisation?," in Evers, A., Nowotny, H. and Wintersberger, H. (eds.) *The Changing Face of Welfare*, Aldershot: Gower Publishing Company Limited.

Walsham, G. (2001) *Making a World of Difference: IT in a Global Context*, Chichester: Wiley.

Wheen, F. (2004) *How Mumbo-Jumbo Conquered the World: A Short History of Modern Delusions*, London: Fourth Estate.

Williams, S.J. and Bendelow, G.B. (1998) "Emotions in Social Life: Mapping the Sociological Terrain," in Bendelow, G. B. and Williams, S.J. (eds.) *Emotions in Social Life: Critical Themes and Contemporary Issues*, London: Routledge.

Williamson, G.M. (2005) "Aging Well: Outlook for the 21st Century," in Snyder, C.R. and Lopez, S.J. (eds.) *Handbook of Positive Psychology*, Oxford: Oxford University Press.

Willmott, H. (1993) Strength is Ignorance; Slavery is Freedom: Managing Culture in Modern Organisations," *Journal of Management Studies*, 30(4): 515–52.

Wright, B.A. and Lopez, S.J. (2005) "Widening the Diagnostic Focus," in Snyder, C.R. and Lopez, S.J. (eds) *Handbook of Positive Psychology*, Oxford: Oxford University Press.

Index